Paven Virk

The Usual Auntijies

Methuen Drama

Published by Methuen Drama 2011

1 3 5 7 9 10 8 6 4 2

Methuen Drama
A & C Black Publishers Limited
36 Soho Square
London W1D 3QY
www.methuendrama.com

Extract from *Shirley Valentine* by Willy Russell © Willy Russell
Reproduced, with permission, from *Shirley Valentine and One for the Road* by
Willy Russell (London: Methuen, 1988)

ISBN: 978 1 408 15217 1

Available in the USA from Bloomsbury Academic & Professional, 175 Fifth
Avenue/3rd Floor, New York, NY 10010. www.BloomsburyAcademicUSA.com

A CIP catalogue record for this book is available from the British Library

Typeset by DC Graphic Design Ltd, Swanley Village, Kent

The Usual Auntijies
by Paven Virk

First performance presented on Saturday 5 March 2011
at the Belgrade Theatre, Coventry

Coventry City Council

Supported by
**ARTS COUNCIL
ENGLAND**

THIS PROJECT IS BEING
PART-FUNDED BY THE
EUROPEAN COMMUNITY

Supported by
The National Lottery
through the Heritage Lottery Fund

heritage
lottery fund

LOTTERY FUNDED

The Usual Auntijies

by Paven Virk

Cast (in order of appearence)

Shalini Peiris	Gurpreet
Jamila Massey	Aunty 4
Mamta Kaash	Aunty 2
Shelley King	Aunty 5
Pushpinder Chani	Raj
Paven Virk	Writer

Production Team

Barry Kyle	Director
Mark Bailey	Designer
Nick Beadle	Lighting Designer
Ilona Sekacz	Sound Designer
Arnim Friess	Audio Visual Designer
Jasvir Kang	Poet / Radio Presenter

The Usual Auntijies runs at the Belgrade Theatre Coventry from Saturday 5 March to Saturday 26 March 2011

Cast

Shalini Peiris
Gurpreet

Shalini trained as an actor at Arts Educational after obtaining a BSc degree at the University of London. At Arts Educational Shalini appeared in a range of productions including **The Laramie Project**, **The Secret Rapture**, **Death And The Ploughman**, **Macbeth** and **Paradise Lost**.

Theatre credits include:
Mocha – rehearsed reading (Arcola Theatre); **Lotus Beauty** and **Zindabad** (Tamasha Theatre at The Gate) and **The House Of Bilquis Bibi** (Tamasha – Hampstead Theatre & tour).

Film credits include:
It's Not A Game (short film).

Jamila Massey
Aunty 4

Jamila Massey was born in Simla and emigrated to England at the age of twelve, subsequently graduating from King's College London. She has been the subject of Terry Wogan's **Pause For Thought** and the BBC's **First Light** interviews and in 2005 was the recipient of the Nazia Hassan Foundation Lifetime Achievement Award. Along with her husband Reginald Massey, she has written books on the classical music and dance of India as well as a novel.

Theatre credits include:
Chaos & Calcutta Kosher (Kali Theatre / Theatre Royal Stratford East); **Women Of The Dust** (Tamasha Theatre / Bristol Old Vic); **The Life & Loves Of Mr. Patel** (Leicester Haymarket); **Song For A Sanctuary** (Kali Theatre / Lyric Hammersmith); **The Great Celestial Cow** (Royal Court); **Conduct Unbecoming** (tour of Canada and the UK) and **Moti Roti Puttli Chunni** (Theatre Royal Stratford East / International Tour).

Television credits include:
Coronation Street (Granada Television); **Crash** (BBC Wales); **Chucklevision** (CBBC); **All About Me** (Celador / BBC); **Doctors** and **EastEnders** (BBC); **The Cappuccino Years** (Tiger Aspect Productions); **Casualty** (BBC); **Perfect World** (Tiger Aspect Productions); **Family Pride** (Carlton); **Albion Market** (ITV); **Langley Bottom** (Yorkshire Television); **Churchill's People** (BBC); **Pie In The Sky** (Select TV / BBC); **The Jewel In The Crown** (Granada Television) and **Mind Your Language** (LWT).

Film credits include:
Arabian Nights (Hallmark Productions); **Madame Sousatzka** (Cineplex-Odeon Films); **Chicken Tikka Masala** (Seven Spice Productions); **King Of Bollywood** (Bollywood / iDream Productions); **Wild West** (Channel Four Films); **Distant Mirage** (Distant Mirage Films) and **Sink The Bismarck!** (Twentieth Century Fox Film Company).

Radio credits include:
Over 250 credits for the BBC, including the regular roles of Auntie Satya in **The Archers** and Poornima in **Westway**.

Mamta Kaash
Aunty 2

Theatre credits include:
Journey To The West (Tara Arts); **Ma** (Royal Court); **Moti Roti Puttli Chunni** (Stratford East) and **Heer In London** (Stratford East - Black Theatre Festival).

Film and television credits include:
Shalom Salaam – Best Actress Award, Cannes and **Casualty** (BBC); **Emmerdale** (Yorkshire Television); **River City** (BBC Scotland); **Angels** (BBC); **Pot Boiler Play** (Channel 4); **Dream Child Play** (Crucial Films Channel 4); **Pravina's Wedding** (Central); **Baby Father Serial** (BBC 2); **Crossroads** (Carlton); **Last Rights** (Channel 4); **Dangerfield** and **EastEnders** (BBC); **Animal Ark** (Channel 4); **Hetty Wainthropp Investigates**, **Back Up** and **Between The Lines Series** (BBC); **Inspector Wexford** (ITV); **Learn English** (Finland TV); **Eastern Eye** (BBC); **Lord Mountbatten: The Last Viceroy** (George Walker Productions) and **Tomorrow's World** (BBC).

Radio credits include:
Shanti, **Song Of The Forest**, **Mutiny On The Bounty**, **Bible Readings** and **Bhagvat Gita** (BBC Radio 4); **Petrella Series** (BBC Radio 5); **Night Runners Of Bengal**, **Kipling In Love**, **Shot In The Dark**, **Stitched Up**, **Nauch Girls**, **Singing And Dancing In Kanpur**, **Carpace**, **The Happy Auntie**, **Zinnan Tower** and **Kurdish Play** (BBC Radio 4).

Shelley King
Aunty 5

Theatre credits include:
In The Further Soil (Sampad / International Tour); **Behzti** (Soho Theatre); **Jungantor** (Finborough Theatre); **Free Outgoing** (Royal Court London / Traverse Theatre Edinburgh); **Free Outgoing** (Royal Court); **The Man Of Mode** (National Theatre); **Asian Woman Talk Back** and **Paper Thin** (Kali Theatre); **Nathan The Wise** (Hampstead Theatre); **Chaos** (Kali Theatre); **Behtzi** (Birmingham Repertory Theatre); **Hobson's Choice** (Young Vic Theatre); **Bombay Dreams** (The Really Useful Theatre Company); **Calcutta Kosher** (Kali Theatre); **Besharam** (Soho Theatre / Birmingham Repertory Theatre); **River On Fire** (Kali Theatre); **Macbeth** (Theatre Unlimited); **The Crutch** (The Royal Court); **A Midsummer Night's Dream** (Tara Arts); **Orpheus** (Actors Touring Company); **Dance Like A Man** (Tara Arts / Leicester Haymarket); **Top Girls** (Royal Theatre Northampton); **Damon and Pythias** (Shakespeare Globe Theatre); **A Modern Husband** (Actors Touring Company); **Women of Troy** (National Theatre); **Ion** (Actors Touring Company); **Death and the Maiden** (New Wolsey Theatre); **Heer Ranjha** (Tara Arts); **Little Clay Cart** (National Theatre); **Cloud 9** (Contact, Manchester); **Tartuffe** (National Theatre); **Mohair** and **The Burrow** (The Royal Court) and **The Innocent Mistress** (Derby Playhouse).

Film and television credits include:
Rafta Rafta (Left Bank Pictures); **Code 46** (Revolution Films); **The Bill** (Talkback Thames); **Silent Witness**, **Banglatown Banquet**, **Twisted Tales** and **Silent Witness** (BBC); **See How They Run** (BBC TV / ABC TV); **Tandoori Nights** (Picture Palace); **Real Women, A Secret Slave, King of The Ghetto**, **Angels** and **Holby City** (BBC) and **The Jewel in the Crown** (Granada TV).

Radio credits include:
Mr Anwar's Farewell To Stornoway, **Reunion With Rama** and **The Spiritual Centre** (BBC Radio 4) and **The Goddess** (The Watershed Partnership).

Pushpinder Chani Raj

Theatre credits include: **Wuthering Heights** and **14 Songs, Two Weddings and A Funeral** (Tamasha Theatre); **A Thin Red Line** and **Dead Eye** (Kali Theatre / Birmingham Repertory Theatre); **What We Did To Weinstein** (Menier Chocolate Factory); **Twelfth Night** (Stage Work Co.); **Paper Thin** (Kali Theatre); **Midnight's Children** (RSC); **Made In India** (Leicester Haymarket); **Baiju Bawra** (Theatre Royal Stratford East); **Momentum Festival** (Curve Theatre) and **Transmissions Festival** (Birmingham Repertory Theatre).

Film and television credits include: **Ashes** (Windward Films); **Fair City**, **Almost Adult** (Parallex); **Life Isn't All Ha Ha Hee Hee** (Hat Trick); **Doctors** and **Casualty** (BBC); **Fantasy Movies, Cross My Heart** (Film Four) and **Anita & Me** (Starfield Productions).

Radio credits include: **Concrete Jungle**, **Ties**, **A Minus**, **Silver Street**, **Behind Closed Doors**, **Reality Check**, **We're Not Getting Married** and **Resolutions** (BBC Radio).

Paven Virk
Writer

Named as one of Screen International's "Stars of Tomorrow" 2010, Paven has been part of the Royal Court Young Writers Programme, the NFTS Screenwriting for Film & TV Course and the Theatre Royal Stratford East Musical Theatre Writing Residency. She founded her own Second Generation Theatre Company at 17 and co-produced **Girlie Talk** and **Boy Meets Girl** with the Belgrade Theatre before taking a break and returning to writing full time two years ago. Paven completed a 10 week writing attachment with The National Theatre Studio in 2009 and is currently under commission to the Tricycle Theatre in London to write a new full-length play.

She is working with Mike Elliot on a film set in Coventry currently entitled **3 Minute Heroes**, which recently was included on this year's prestigious Brit List. She is also developing a screenplay called **Queen of the Steering Wheel**, a screenplay with BAFTA winning director Martina Amati & Cowboy Films currently entitled **East** and a film called **Give Me An C.H.E.E.R** with Mandalay Vision in the US. For television she is developing an original series and a single film commissioned by Hillbilly Films for the BBC.

Theatre credits include:
Too Young to Remember (Belgrade Theatre); **Borders** (Tricycle Theatre); **The Boy and the Dog Who Walked to the Moon** (Edinburgh Festival, Pleasance Theatre) and **Who You Calling a Superhero?** (Heat & Light Company, Hampstead Theatre).

Production Team

Barry Kyle
Director

Barry Kyle is an Honorary Associate Director of the Royal Shakespeare Company and Founding Artistic Director of Swine Palace Productions in Louisiana. He was the first Artistic Director of the RSC's Swan Theatre in Stratford-upon-Avon. Mr. Kyle has directed more than 30 productions for the Royal Shakespeare Company. These include **Love's Labour's Lost**, **Measure for Measure**, **The Two Noble Kinsmen**, **The Taming of the Shrew**, **Richard II**, Edward Bond's **Lear**, and Marlowe's **Dr. Faustus**. His work has been seen in London, Paris, Berlin, Vienna, Jerusalem, Moscow, Warsaw, Melbourne, Singapore and many other places around the world.

He has been twice nominated for Olivier Awards as Best Director for his RSC productions of Shakespeare's comedies in London. In New York he directed an off-Broadway production of **Henry V**, which was awarded the Lucille Lortel Award for Best Revival. He also directed **To Kill a Mockingbird** at Actor's Theatre of Louisville and **Romeo and Juliet** at the Shakespeare Theatre in Washington, D.C. In New York City, he adapted and directed **Henry VI**, which won a Drama Desk Nomination as Outstanding Revival.

He was the first Western director to work at the National Theatre in Prague where he directed Shakespeare's **King Lear** during the 'velvet revolution'. Mr. Kyle later directed a ground-breaking all-female production of **Richard III** at Shakespeare's Globe in London, where he had also directed a production of **King Lear**, which went on to play in Tokyo, Japan.

In 2006, he directed **The Mysteries** – a modern version of the medieval Christian drama, set in the medieval cathedral in Coventry, for the Belgrade Theatre. *The Guardian* ranked the production as one of that year's 5 star productions in England, and he was awarded "Director of the Year" by Britain's Daily Mail newspaper in 2006. In 2007, Mr. Kyle directed Shakespeare's **A Midsummer Night's Dream** in a big budget production in Singapore on a hillside site, with a primarily Asian cast, and in which the set covered five acres. He has directed the English and Welsh premiere of **The Drawer Boy** at Clwyd Theatre Cymru.

In 2011 he revives **Oh What A Lovely War** in the USA at the National World War 1 Monument and Museum in Kansas City. He is also directing Ron Hutchinson's new adaptation of **They Shoot Horses Don't They**, again in America.

Mark Bailey
Designer

Mark read Drama at the University of Hull and then studied Theatre Design at Croydon College of Art, since then he has designed over 150 productions in Britain and worldwide.

Theatre design includes:
Legal Fictions, Rent, Mack and Mabel, Rat Pack Confidential, The Importance of Being Earnest (also Toronto), **The Winslow Boy, Iolanthe, The Gondoliers,** costumes for **Present Laughter** and **Which Witch** (all West End); **Jekyll and Hyde the Musical** (National Tour); **Hamlet** and **Macbeth** (Chicago); **The Pretenders** (Oslo); **Privates on Parade** (West Yorkshire Playhouse / Birmingham Repertory Theatre); **The Double Dealer** and **The Seagull** (Gate Theatre, Dublin); **Polygraph** (Nottingham Playhouse) and national tours of **The Rivals, Look Back in Anger, A Chorus of Disapproval, Hadrian VII, Peace In Our Time, Entertaining Mr. Sloane, A Judgment in Stone** and **To Kill A Mockingbird.** Musical theatre includes **Fiddler on the Roof, Cabaret** and **Irma La Douce** (Watermill Theatre Newbury); **Babes in Arms** (Cardiff International Music Festival) and **The Threepenny Opera** (National Theatre).

Opera and dance design includes:
Madama Butterfly (Nevill Holt / Grange Park); **The Sleeping Beauty** (Hong Kong Ballet); **The Snow Queen** and **Melody on the Move** (English National Ballet); **Varii Capricci** for **The Wright Occasion** (in celebration of Peter Wright's 80th birthday); **L'Arlesienne** (English National Ballet School); **Rise and Fall of the City of Mahagonny** (LA Opera); **Ariadne Auf Naxos** (Opera de Lausanne and Maggio Musical Florence) and **Carmen** (ROH Linbury), as well as productions for Buxton Festival, Opera North and Almeida Opera.

Mark is an Associate Artist at Clwyd Theatr Cymru, where credits include **Pieces** (also Brits off Broadway, New York), **A Child's Christmas, Taming of the Shrew, Gaslight, To Kill a Mockingbird, A Glass Menagerie, Shakespeare's Will, Pygmalion, Great Expectations, A Midsummer Night's Dream, Equus, King Lear, Private Lives, Present Laughter, Hay Fever, Blithe Spirit,** and **One Flew Over the Cuckoo's Nest.** He has also worked at Bristol Old Vic, Theatre Royal Plymouth, Theatre Royal York, Birmingham Repertory Theatre, Glasgow Citz, Oxford Playhouse and Chichester Festival Theatre.

Television design includes:
Broken Lives (BBC2).

Nick Beadle
Lighting Designer

Design credits for Birmingham Repertory Theatre include: Dancing at Lughnasa, Shakespeare's Will, Festen, Great Expectations, The Drawer Boy, Drowned Out, A Midsummer Night's Dream, A Toy Epic, Porth y Byddar, Of Mice and Men, Home Front, Waiting for Godot, Portrait of the Artist as a Young Dog, Hosts of Rebecca, Happy End, Song of the Earth, Art, The Devils, The Rose Tattoo, The Rape of the Fair Country, Dick Whittington, Silas Marner, Sweeney Todd, The Threepenny Opera, Hard Times, A View from the Bridge, Aladdin, Cinderella and Robin Hood (also Clwyd Theatr Cymru); Elizabeth Rex, Racing Demon, Murmuring Judges, The Absence of War, Krindlekraxx, Private Lives and Closer.

Design credits for Theatre by the Lake, Keswick include: Northanger Abbey, What the Butler Saw, Bus Stop, Arsenic and Old Lace, The Lady In the Van, A Midsummer Night's Dream, Summer Lightning, The Borrowers, Chorus of Disapproval, The Importance of Being Earnest, The Hired Man, Dick Barton – Special Agent!, Gaslight, Les Liaisons Dangereuses, Sinbad! – The Untold Tale, Of Mice and Men, Portraits in Song, The Mother, Habeas Corpus, Mrs Warren's Profession, The Hired Man, The Real Inspector Hound, The Woman in Black, All My Sons, The Good Companions, Tenant of Wildfell Hall, Blithe Spirit, Season's Greetings, The Snow Queen and The Wizard of Oz.

Other design credits include: And All the Children Cried (West Yorkshire Playhouse); Breaking the Code (Chester Gateway); Mata Hari (Watford Palace); Sweeney Todd, Perfect Days, Double Indemnity, Neville's Island, A Family Affair, A Mad World, My Masters, Cinderella and Dick Whittington (New Wolsey Theatre, Ipswich); Angels Rave On, Double Indemnity, Anatol (Nottingham Playhouse); Inner City Jam, Heaven Can Wait and The Mother (all national tours); The Guardsman (The Churchill, Bromley, tour and the Albery Theatre); The Gift (Birmingham Repertory Theatre/ The Tricycle Theatre); A Wedding Story (Birmingham Repertory Theatre, tour and the Soho); Mrs. Warren's Profession (Royal Exchange Theatre); Breaking The Code (Chester Gateway); A Streetcar Named Desire (Bristol Old Vic); China Song (Clear Day Productions tour and Plymouth Theatre Royal); Vita and Virginia (Sphinx); The Alchemical Wedding, The Merchant of Venice, Romeo and Juliet, The Cherry Orchard, Racing Demon, The Rehearsal, The Double Inconstancy and Noises Off (Salisbury Playhouse); The Life of Galileo, The Resistible Rise of Arturo Ui, The Herbal Bed, Arcadia, Amy's View, Who's Afraid of Virginia Woolfe? and Pygmalion (Library Theatre, Manchester); Killing Time (national tour); Shirley Valentine (national tour); Suzanna Andler and Hedda Garbler (Chichester and tour); Vertigo (Guildford); Watching the Sand From the Sea (Derby Playhouse); Tosca (Opera Holland Park); The Marriage of Figaro (English Touring Opera); The Canterbury Tales (Garrick Theatre); Old Times (Wyndham's Theatre); From The Mississippi Delta and Full Moon (Young Vic); Jane Eyre (Playhouse Theatre); Lady Audley's Secret and The Broken Heart (Lyric Hammersmith); A Midsummer Night's

Dream and **The Tempest** (City of London Festival); **Gaslight**, **The Piggy Bank**, **A Country Girl**, **Marie Lloyd** and **Perfect Days** (Greenwich Theatre); **A Better Day** and **Waiting to Inhale** (Theatre Royal Stratford East); **You be Ted and I'll be Sylvia** (Hampstead Theatre); **Hymn to Love – Homage to Piaf** (Drill Hall); **The Guardsman** (Albery Theatre); **A Busy Day** (Lyric Hammersmith); **Women of Troy** and **The Threepenny Opera** (National Theatre).

Ilona Sekacz
Sound Designer

Ilona Sekacz has written many musical scores for theatre, film and television. Her more recent work includes the creation of 'soundscapes', which combine music, voices and sound effects.

Theatre scores include:
A Midsummer Night's Dream (RSC / Broadway); **Les Liaisons Dangereuses**, **The Jew of Malta**, **Twelfth Night**, **King Lear**, **The Beggar's Opera**, **The Trojans**, **A Winter's Tale** and **Romeo and Juliet** (RSC); **Major Barbara**, **Burnt by the Sun**, **Saint Joan** and **The Cherry Orchard** (National Theatre) and **Onassis** (Novello Theatre, West End).

Television scores include:
Northanger Abbey, **Boys from the Blackstuff**, **The Insurance Man** – BAFTA nomination, **Dalziel and Pascoe** and **Mortimer's Law** – BAFTA award (BBC).

Film scores include:
Mrs. Dalloway and **Antonia's Line** – Oscar for Best Foreign Film (Bergen Films); **Solomon and Gaenor** – Oscar nomination for Best Foreign Film and **Wondrous Oblivion** (APT Film and Television) and **Elena's Gift** – St. Malo Film Festival Award for Best Musical Score (Zephyr Films).

Arnim Friess
Audio Visual Designer

Arnim trained and worked as a photographer and audio-visual media designer in his native Germany, before moving to the UK to study Scenography, receiving an MA at Birmingham Institute of Art and Design. He is the founder member of Pixelbox Ltd, which specialises in designing dynamic performance environments, blending media like lighting, slide and video projection, animation, film-making and graphic design. His lighting and projections have been seen not only in theatres around the world, but also in a zoo, a monastery, an abandoned pub and deep down in a cave in the Forest of Dean. Performances in the UK, China, Canada, the USA, Ireland, India, the Netherlands, Germany, Italy, Portugal and Denmark have spanned diverse arts forms from theatre to opera and ballet via puppetry, Indian dance, experimental music and children's shows.

Recent designs include **Too Much Pressure** and **We Love You City** (Belgrade Theatre); **Space Odyssey** (Orchestra of the Swan) and **Forever in your Debt** (with Foursight Theatre) for Talking Birds. For Blue Eyed Soul Dance Company: **Wander** (Hong Kong) and **Take** (Washington D.C.). **The Long Road** (The Curve, Leicester); **Lucky Seven** (Hampstead Theatre); **The Death of Harry Leon** (Ouroborus Theatre Dublin) and the National Holocaust Memorial Day in Coventry. **One Night in November; The Dark Side of Buffoon; Monged; Puntila and His Man Matti** and the **Mysteries** for the Belgrade Theatre Coventry. **The Suicide** and **An Inspector Calls** (Theatr Clwyd) and **The White Album** (Nottingham Playhouse).

Past designs have been science-fiction opera **The Pitchshifter** for leading

Dutch contemporary music ensemble Insomnia, award winning **Rumblefish, Looking for JJ, Road** and **Lord of the Flies** for Pilot Theatre, bricks-in-space spectacle **Life on Mars** (Legolands worldwide), the appearance of hundreds of angels inside St Paul's Cathedral for the City of London Festival, Joe Guy (Soho Theatre); **The Saint of Bleecker Street** (Peacock Theatre West End); **Amour** for Oval Theatre London and the Dance-Centre Toronto, **Mine, Moll Flanders, Metropolis** and **The Importance of Being Earnest** (Kaos Theatre); **Paradise** (Birmingham Rep); **Angels in America** (Sheffield Crucible); **Oliver** (Liverpool Playhouse); Mozart's **Mass in C-minor** (Birmingham Royal Ballet); Hanif Kureishi's **My Beautiful Laundrette** (Snap Theatre); **The Wall, King** and Philipp Glass' **Satyagraha** (Midlands Arts Centre); Bryony Lavery's **Shot Through the Heart** (Pentabus Theatre) and **Hard Day's Night** (Hull Truck Theatre Company).

Arnim also works as a photographer and graphic designer and lives in Warwickshire with his wife Susanne, daughters Ella and Amelie, and an overly dramatic cat. He enjoys playing drums and experimental cooking for fearless friends.

Jasvir Kang
Poet / Radio Presenter

Jasvir Kang was born in Punjab, North India. During her time in India, she trained as a visual artist but it wasn't until she arrived in England during the late 1960s, that she realised her real creative passion was writing.

Jasvir spent the 1970s writing short stories and poems, reflecting her own experiences and the lives of South Asian women she knew. The stories spoke about the oppression and intolerances experienced by some women and the impact this was having on their family life.

By the late 1980s Jasvir had established herself as a confident writer within some sections of the South Asian literature community in the UK. In 1989, her first book of short stories called **Geji** was published. A further three more books were published in the 1990s.

By the early 1990s, Jasvir began to seek new methods of reaching diverse audiences including pursuing a career in radio broadcasting. This led to her first presenting job on a Coventry (UK) based South Asian radio station called Radio Harmony. This followed presenting work with Radio BBC WM and Radio Sangam. By the late 1990s Jasvir had established herself as a popular presenter on Radio XL (Birmingham, UK), where she discussed challenging topics and shared her poetry and stories with the listeners.

The two other areas that have supported Jasvir to reach a diverse audience are her involvement in the performing arts as an actress / workshop facilitator (including work with Men Mela Theatre, Multi Arts Nation, Reminiscence Theatre, Pangran Theatre, Kali Theatre and the Belgrade Theatre) and the production of her two CDs featuring her short stories and poetry.

The poem **Dolli** is heard on Jasvir's radio show in **The Usual Auntijies**. The poem was carefully selected from her 40 or so poems due to its subject matter, which strongly complimented the issues of the play.

Jasvir is now with Ambur radio where she presents her Punjabi programme.

"Dolli"- in olden days an Indian bride was sent to her husband's house in a wooden carriage called Dolli.

"Dolli"
(Palanquin*)

Once you have been sent in the Dolli
to you husband's house,
do not leave the house until you die.
We will have peace of mind only if we
could see
your dead body carried out from that
house in a coffin.

Treat your mother in-law as your own
mother
even if she does not allow you to have
food more than once a day.
Always respect her by bowing to her
even if she beats you up and breaks
your bones.

Treat your father in-law as your own
father,
even if he tries to touch you with sexual
desires.
Do not let anyone have even slightest
idea about his behaviour, my daughter!
because that is how you will be faithful
to them.

Treat your sister-in-law as your own
sister
even if she makes your life a hell.
Even when your sister-in-law comes
back from her own in-law's house and
turns her brother (your husband) against
you so to beat you up.

If you could not have a child because
your husband is impotent, take the
blame yourself.
If you are not given enough food, do not
let the whole world know about it (keep
quiet about it).

If you want your parents to live with
dignity
do not give others a chance to lift a
finger towards them even if your life has
finished for you.

Once you have been sent in the Dolli
to you husband's house
do not leave the house until you die.
We will have peace of mind only if we
could see
your dead body carried out from that
house in a coffin.

Jasvir Kang

Belgrade Theatre

The Belgrade Theatre was built in 1958 as part of the reconstruction of Coventry after World War II. Holding 858 in its two-tier main auditorium, it remains one of the largest regional producing theatres in Britain.

The theatre soon became renowned for its programme of exciting new drama and early Company members at the Belgrade included Trevor Nunn, Ian McKellen, Joan Plowright and Leonard Rossiter, with Arnold Wesker and David Turner among the new dramatists.

The theatre remains the major arts and cultural facility in Coventry and the only building-based professional producing theatre company in the city. Autumn 2007 saw the re-opening of the Belgrade after completion of its major capital project, including the creation of a new, flexible 250-300 seat second space, B2, and refurbishment of the existing listed building.

Having started the Theatre-in-Education (TiE) movement in the 1960s the Belgrade also continues to pioneer new initiatives in this field as well as other community and outreach programmes.

The Belgrade creates theatre in the belief that it can enrich its community and fundamentally change peoples' lives for the better.

Under the current Artistic Director and Chief Executive, Hamish Glen, the Theatre's vision is to be one of the most dynamic producing houses in the country and to offer an exciting mix of entertaining and engaging live experiences all under one roof in its newly invigorated building. This mission is expressed by presenting a vibrant programme of produced, visiting and community work in the two auditoria and other spaces that is informed by a distinctive and brave artistic policy designed to attract local and national attention, cater to and develop the different audiences in and around Coventry, lift the profile of the theatre as a producing theatre, bear witness to its community's experiences, find a unique voice for the Belgrade in the context of the region, attract leading theatre artists – in short re-establish the vision, radicalism and internationalism that marked the opening of the theatre in 1958.

Since re-opening, the reinvigorated Belgrade has produced numerous successful productions including Joanna Murray-Smith's adaptation of Ingmar Bergman's **Scenes from a Marriage**, directed by Trevor Nunn, and Alan Pollock's play about the Coventry Blitz, **One Night in November**, directed by Hamish Glen.

For further information please visit www.belgrade.co.uk.

Belgrade Theatre Coventry

Belgrade Theatre Staff List

Introduction: the background of *The Usual Auntijies*

In 1994, a partnership between the Belgrade Theatre and Multi Arts Nation was formed to develop and perform a new play called *Geji*. Jane Hytch at the Belgrade and Hardish Virk from Multi Arts Nation led on the development and management of what was going to become a unique story that had never been told on a Coventry stage before. *Geji* was the name of an Indian woman who was living within a violent marriage. The play dealt with a number of social and political issues that had become so taboo that it was difficult for many to imagine that these actually existed. *Geji* was an adaptation by playwright David Semple from a number of short stories written by Coventry-based writer, Jasvir Kang. The reality of the stories became significantly apparent when during one performance of *Geji* a group of South Asian women started crying in the audience. Some of these women were relating to a scene in the play that depicted the killing of baby girls. As one audience member would explain later, 'Girls were seen as a burden and many families would wish for a son. It was better to kill the girls at birth than pass the burden on to their daughters.'

Geji was a powerful, challenging and emotional play that was popular with both audiences and critics and sold out at the Belgrade Studio in 1995.

The original idea of *The Usual Auntijies* was to pick up from *Geji* so as to create new work that tells stories of people in our communities that are rarely given a voice on British stages.

The initial stages for *The Usual Auntijies* started in 2005, when the Belgrade Theatre commissioned Multi Arts Nation to research and develop a new play to perform in the new Belgrade 2 space and one that was born out of Coventry. Hardish Virk recruited Jasvir Kang (writer and broadcaster) and emerging playwright Paven Virk to facilitate storytelling workshops with a diverse range of South Asian women's community groups based in Coventry. These groups met with Jasvir and Paven in confidential and safe environments and they were supported to share and listen to each other's stories.

The findings of these workshops led to Paven writing a synopsis, which became the basis of the script for *The Usual Auntijies*. The script has been through a number of stages including a week-long development programme led by Anthony Clarke (during his time as the Artistic Director of Hampstead Theatre, London), which was followed by a reading by professional actors to a private audience. Another professional reading of the play took place at the Herbert Art Gallery, Coventry in February 2009, to an enthusiastic public audience who were keen to see a stage production of *The Usual Auntijies*.

The Usual Auntijies is definitely a story from the mind and heart of Paven Virk – as a writer she has been fully committed to the play since its inception and has continued this passion throughout the Belgrade production. Jasvir Kang is also integral not only to the early development stages of the play, but to the spirit of the play.

Jasvir has been a writer of short stories and poetry in Punjabi since the 1980s and she was among a handful of South Asian female poets who would be invited to South Asian literature events (1980s–1990s) that would on the whole attract mainly South Asian men as audiences and artists. On many occasions Jasvir would be heckled by the male-dominated audience when she spoke about subjects such as domestic violence and forced marriages as there seemed to be a reluctance to accept that these took place within the South Asian communities or that they should be aired within a public space. Jasvir would continue her readings over the shouting coming from the audience and then leave the stage with her head held high. No matter how challenging and sometimes abusive the situation became, Jasvir continued with a spirit that is captured in the play. A spirit of hope, change and solidarity.

The journey of *The Usual Auntijies* has involved many individuals who have contributed to the creative and authentic voice of the play. Therefore we would like to thank the following individuals for their contribution and support.

Partners involved in the development of this play have included Multi Arts Nation Ltd, Imagineer Productions, Belgrade Theatre and Hampstead Theatre. Particular thanks are due to Hamish Glen for realising this play's vision as a Belgrade Production, Jane Hytch for her ongoing support since the early 1990s, Anthony Clarke and Frances Poet for their expertise in developing the play.

Hardish Virk

Paven Virk

The Usual Auntijies

Author's Preface

On one particular workshop reading for *The Usual Auntjies*, one of the actresses took me aside and said, 'I cannot believe I am reading about my life.' I asked her which bits she meant, and she replied, 'I am Aunty 2, that is all I can say.' I mention this as Aunty 2 to me is the voice that is rarely heard. She is the woman we pass sitting on a bench or waiting at a bus stop, dressed in her traditional outfit and avoiding any eye contact. She looks like all the other South Asian women who must have come here with certain expectations, of a new life, an adoring husband, children, many friends and a chance to share stories of where they came from and to learn about where they had arrived. For some, certain aspects have been realised but for others these expectations have been shattered. Until the day Jasvir and I attended a workshop in a community centre in Coventry where a group of elderly South Asian women much like Aunty 2 were sat, I would not have truly appreciated these women and their stories. I knew from that day that I wanted to give a voice to these women in that room, the Auntijies who sit on a bench while people pass by. I also wanted to work closely with Mandy Sanghera, a human rights activist who had discussed some shocking cases with me regarding forced marriages that I feel demand a lot of support and greater awareness. For these women this is about overcoming the past, accepting the present and creating a future together by transcending their differences and becoming friends.

The Usual Auntijies is something I've been wanting to write for a long time, and the support of my mother Jasvir and my brother Hardish – who both refuse to sit back when it comes to subjects they are passionate about – allowed me to go from a light comedy to a play whose subject matter challenged me as a writer and therefore I hope challenges the audience. I have no idea how it will be received, but I would be more than happy if even one person in the audience were to be inspired by the play.

Paven Virk
January 2011

Acknowledgements

Hardish Virk and Multi Arts Nation, Jane Hytch and Imagineer Productions, Jasvir Kang, Harriet Pennington Legh, Mandy Sanghera, Anthony Clarke and the Hampstead Theatre, Frances Poet, Jittey Samra, Marion Doyen, Nicholas Stokes, Pippa Ellis, Dilwara Begum, Manj, Neil and Lyla, Kathi Leahy, Denise Pitter, Paul Nicholl, Archie Panjabi, Seema Bowri and KIRAN, Asian Women's Aid.

Dedicated to Jasvir Kang, a mother, daughter and a voice of many women who are unable to use theirs. The reaction to Jasvir's poetry about South Asian women has sometimes overwhelmed me. She has the ability to silence a room and fill it with tears of joy, pain and anger as the audience react as if they are the person being spoken about or know of someone in those situations, but most importantly she is living proof that you can start a fresh life at any age, overcoming any obstacles that may come your way.

Characters

Aunty 2, *Storytelling Aunty; an elderly South Asian woman.*
Aunty 4, *Lonely Aunty; an elderly South Asian woman.*
Aunty 5, *Mischievous Aunty; a very striking elderly South Asian woman.*
Gurpreet, *a bride from India.*
Raj, *a British Asian man.*
Jasvir Kang *(voiceover), a Punjabi radio presenter.*

Author's Notes

Speech in italics indicates that Punjabi is being spoken.

Jasvir Kang is a Punjabi poet and radio presenter who uses her poetry to inspire and empower women.

Benji translates as 'sister'; it is a word used between women, even if they are not real sisters, as an affectionate term for each other.

Dolli – in olden days an Indian bride was sent to her husband's house in a wooden carriage called a *dolli*.

Act One

Opening Scene

V/O   *Voices of young girls playing.*

We hear the young girls playing in a field in India. One girl shouts, 'I want to marry a prince and live happily ever after.' It is echoed in different South Asian languages. The voices fade.

Gurpreet (*Indian, girl next door, late teens*) *is sat writing in her diary.*

Gurpreet   It is November and I have had the best week visiting Uncle who said that he has found me a prince, Raj. He will appear on a white horse and take me to his castle, a castle tucked away in faraway Coventry! Uncle says it snows there every day, but my Raj will keep me warm. I will only settle for a someone who holds me as tight as Papa did. Someone who talks to me with a gentle voice, laughs at my silly jokes. Uncle has fulfilled his duty and I shall now fulfil my duty, like Mother did with Papa. I shall write to Mother every week and send her many kisses …

Gurpreet *continues talking while the music starts.*

Spotlight appears on a hand that places a needle on a record player. The hand belongs to **Aunty 5**.

Gurpreet *exits.*

Music   Les Misérables' *'I Dreamed a Dream'* starts to play in the background.

A verse plays over each **Auntijies** *reveal.*

A Spotlight appears on the face of an elderly South Asian woman, **Aunty 4**. *She is sat staring into space.*

A Spotlight comes up on a second elderly South Asian woman, **Aunty 2**. *She is dressed in a (simple) traditional Indian salwar kameez. Her face is scarred with a severe burn mark. Her hair is grey in a low bun. She sits at a table staring at a stack of tinned food. (Spam, corned beef, etc.)*

A Spotlight comes up on a third elderly South Asian woman, **Aunty 5***.
She is dressed in an Indian suit that clashes with her bright modern high
heels. Her grey / black hair is in a low ponytail. She stands in front of a
mirror staring at herself.*

Spotlights fade on **Aunty 2 and Aunty 4***. They exit leaving*
Aunty 5 *alone.*

Music fades.

Scene One

HOUSE NO. 23. LIVING ROOM

It is dark. **Aunty 5** *rushes to the window, gently lifts the curtain and
looks outside. She has a mixture of a Scottish and Indian accent.*

Aunty 5   I know you're there … I can see you. (*Whispers.*) I
can see his eyes … but with you by my side dear, I don't fear his
eyes my dear friend … do I?

She drops the curtain and looks around.

Dear …?

Beat.

Dear?

Beat.

Why did she leave me, Joan?

*She turns a table lamp on; lights come up on a simple living room. There is
a sofa, standing mirror, massage chair, TV, video, payphone, tape recorder
and a small dining table (on the table is a pile of tinned food). On the floor
is a bird cage covered with an emerald sheet and in the corner is a life-size
cardboard cutout of Joan Collins as Alexis from* Dynasty.

Aunty 5 *looks over at a bare wall.*

The clock? Where's the clock?

She walks over to Joan's cutout.

Did you see her take the clock, Joan? Well, did you?
I've a lot to do today, I've … (*Stops herself.*) Why did she take the clock?

She snaps out of her state, sits on the sofa and rummages through her handbag.

(*Mutters*) Just because we don't do anything does not mean we don't require the time. I mean, I need the time, otherwise …

She finds a note. **Aunty 2** *enters and walks straight over to the payphone then clocks* **Aunty 5** *and quietly puts the receiver down. She stands watching unseen by* **Aunty 5**.

(*Reading the note*) The day you release yourself, release the emerald dove.

She screws the note up and shoves it back in her handbag. **Aunty 5** *laughs. An uneasy laugh, practised to conceal any true emotions.*

My dear friend leaves me, takes the clock and gives me a bird! It seems barely alive and I don't think she, the bird, wishes to fly around in this grim world any more. Do you?

She lifts the sheet off the bird cage and drops some food into the cage then covers it again.

Aunty 2 *exits.*

And she claims it is a dove. Not any old dove, but an emerald dove. But, aah, I Googled this so-called *emerald dove* and guess what? Their back and wings are bright emerald green. They are found in the Indian subcontinent, China, South East Asia and even Australia, but not bloody Coventry! She's left me with a green pigeon …

Aunty 2 (*speaking with a strong Indian accent and broken English*) *re-enters making noise and turns the main light on.* **Aunty 5**, *a little startled, quickly sits up and puts the television on.*

Dynasty *theme tune plays.*

Aunty 5   Oh hurry, it's about to start.

Aunty 2 *stands watching.*

People don't really understand her. I do. She is a woman of great strength, power. There should be more women like her.

Beat.

Well, come on.

Aunty 2 *sits next to* **Aunty 5**, *who is engrossed.*

Watch Miss Collins carefully, she really can help you. Look, when she smiles, there's a real sense of what being a woman in a man's world is about.

Aunty 2   She name Joan or Alexis?

Aunty 5   Well, one is who she actually is and the other is who she portrays …

Aunty 2   Por…trays?

Aunty 5   Pretends to be. I adore Alexis, but prefer Joan.

Aunty 2   Ah, so you like Joan.

Beat.

Who is Joan?

Aunty 5   Oh my, give me strength. She …

Aunty 5 *walks up to the cardboard cutout.*

… Is Alexis, but when she goes home she will become Joan. Understand?

Aunty 2 *looks confused.* **Aunty 5** *starts to demonstrate, she glides across the living room pretending to be Joan Collins.*

Aunty 5   Dear, to be *her* (*Points to TV.*) you must be in touch with your masculine and your feminine side, otherwise you'll be defeated. Also, remember stand tall and sit straight. Women in India sit on the floor like animals on a farm and that's not very ladylike, not very ladylike at all. My mother, she was the worst. Whilst Joan, she doesn't walk, she simply glides.

Aunty 2   (*at the TV*) Look, she find out his truth!

Aunty 5   A cheater always gets found out my dear.

Aunty 2   Benji, can I ask something?

Aunty 5   (*at the TV*) Oh, here she goes!

Aunty 2   You no been sleeping?

Beat.

Aunty 5   I … just came down for a glass of water.

Aunty 2 *carries on looking at* **Aunty 5** *who does not wish to reveal her truth of not being able to sleep and snaps back.*

Improving your English is a concern, my sleep patterns, not your concern. I hardly need the beauty sleep. Now, listen carefully, soon you'll be able to form an intelligent sentence.

They carry on watching for a bit.

Anyway, why are you up so early?

Aunty 2   I … er … do big clean today.

Aunty 5   (*suspicious*) Really? The place looks pretty clean to me.

They are both lying, they both clock this. **Aunty 2** *exits.* **Aunty 5** *takes off her heels, grabs some red nail varnish and starts to paint her toenails.* **Aunty 2** *re-enters hoovering the floor.*

Aunty 2   Could you pass me my toe dryer?

Aunty 2 *does not hear.* **Aunty 5** *attempts to walk on her heels over to the dining table where she picks up a small toe dryer and makes her way back to the sofa.*

Aunty 2 *finishes, exits and re-enters with a plate of sausage and green mash. Just as* **Aunty 5** *is about to start drying her toes* **Aunty 2** *loudly places the plate down on the table.*

Aunty 2   Breakfast!

Aunty 5 *sighs and makes her way to the table, with toe dryer in hand.*

Aunty 5   The mash, it's green.

Aunty 2   Nice green hunah?

Aunty 5   Different.

Aunty 2   I make yesterday, but you not feel like eating. You too upset your Benji friend leave.

Aunty 2 *takes a cleaning note and places a bottle of Mr Muscle on the table.*

You no read cleaning list?

Aunty 5   Sorry?

Aunty 2   You no clean oven.

Aunty 5   I've been busy.

Aunty 2   You never leave house. How you busy?

Aunty 5   If it wasn't for my savings you wouldn't be using decent cleaning products so please don't suggest that I don't contribute!

Aunty 5 *takes a mouthful of mash and coughs it back out.*

Aunty 2   Curry mash.

Aunty 5   I wish you would warn me before you experiment with the food. I can't eat it.

Aunty 2 *looks upset.*

Aunty 2   Well, I try something new tomorrow.

Aunty 5   Sorry … It's the chilli. I don't like too much chilli.

Aunty 5 *picks up a tin of Spam from* **Aunty 2***'s pile of tins.*

There's not much you can do with Spam. Why don't you make some of our friend's favourite food.

Aunty 2   Saag?

Aunty 5   In memory of her. She simply adored your saag.

Aunty 5 *takes some money out of her purse.*

Here, buy some spinach, organic.

Aunty 2 *looks at the money and shakes her head, she then picks up a large food parcel off the floor and puts it on the table.*

You mustn't carry it by yourself, it's too heavy.

Aunty 2   I okay. I am very strong.

Aunty 5 *places the money on the table.*

Aunty 5   Take it … please.

Aunty 2   But it your savings. I cannot …

Aunty 5   Dear, we've both had very different opportunities in this country. I have money and you … well … don't.

Aunty 2   I will find job and then have my own business.

Aunty 5   One at a time I think. Anyway, I can help you realise your dream of a business. Myself and my husband had our own business. We were quite successful, but, do you know something? All the money in the world couldn't buy me the taste of your homemade saag.

Aunty 2 *smiles.* **Aunty 5** *offers the money again.*

Please …

Aunty 2 *reluctantly takes it.*

Maybe I'll come to the church with you. I may even stop off at the park.

Aunty 2 *exits with the dishes.*

It would be rather nice, Joan, to sit and watch other people's lives go by. Surely I can't sit here every day watching my own go …

Aunty 5 *puts on her pink stiletto heels, grabs her handbag, fake fur coat and exits.*

SDFX   *We hear the front door open, traffic noise and people.*

Moments later **Aunty 5** *re-enters, closes the living-room door behind her and leans against it dazed.*

(*Whispers*) Tomorrow.

She drops her handbag and bends down to pick it up then clocks her toes.

Oh dear.

She rushes over to the sofa and gently takes off her heels. Checks her toenails for smudges, satisfied that there are none, and admires her feet.

Aunty 2 *enters holding a pink polkadot umbrella.*

My toes look like they belong to a woman half my age. That's what my dear used to say whilst painting my toenails.

Aunty 2   Benji say that?

Aunty 5   Yes, don't you remember? We talked all the time and now she's no longer here.

Aunty 2 *starts to put her coat on.*

Oh, I've asked Rhani for a new door.

Aunty 2   There something wrong with old one?

Aunty 5   We don't want to lose another. Do you know she slept with a knife under her pillow? And now who knows …

Aunty 2 *sits next to* **Aunty 5** *and comforts her.*

Aunty 2   Benji please, she no die.

Aunty 5   We know that for a fact do we!?! She wouldn't just leave me.

Aunty 2   It hard say goodbye to friend.

Aunty 5   She must have been kidnapped! He must have found out she lived here, pulled up in his taxi, pretended to be waiting for someone and once she left the house, grabbed and gagged her, straight into his car.

Aunty 2   Rhani work here, she know everything and she no say Benji was kidnapped.

Aunty 5 *spots the umbrella.*

Aunty 5   That's mine!

Aunty 2   I borrow brelly.

Aunty 5   Brelly?

Aunty 2   Weather lady say it rain.

Aunty 5   I don't care what the weather lady says. That is my *brolly*!

Aunty 5 *almost childlike snatches the umbrella off* **Aunty 2**.

Why didn't you fetch your own things!?!

Aunty 2   You know I was in hospital. How I get things? Huh? How?

There is a moment of silence.

Aunty 5   You're safe now.

Aunty 2   He burn my outside, not my inside.

Aunty 5   True. But I must say, your face is … well it needs … I can't say I know what it's like to have the contents of a chip pan thrown at me, but I sure know how to cover it up!

Aunty 5 *picks up a wooden box with compartments. She opens it and a dancing ballerina appears twirling to some crackly music. She opens one compartment which contains her makeup.*

They sit together.

That my dear is Bella, Bella the ballerina. She belonged to the daughter of an elegant English lady visiting Calcutta. I sat watching the girl playing with her from my rooftop. Hours went by until finally she became bored with her new toy and left her on the pavement. I've never run down my stairs so fast, just so I could rescue her.

Aunty 2 *touches the ballerina and smiles.*

Oh, careful. She's very old. I'm getting her repaired. No one likes a damaged ballerina.

Aunty 2 *freely allows* **Aunty 5** *to touch her face, almost as if it is not hers.* **Aunty 5** *attempts to cover up the scar with concealer but becomes nervous and starts to tremble.*

It starts to rain.

Dear me. What a mess he's made eh? You know you have quite good skin if it wasn't for …

Aunty 5 *turns away upset and starts to look through her makeup.*

Right Max Factor? Oh … I'm running a bit low. Could you get some for me next time you're in town? I'll give you the money of course.

Aunty 5 *puts more makeup on* **Aunty 2** *but it is not covering up the scar.*

Gosh … he's done a darned good job on you.

Aunty 5 *starts to pack away her makeup, taking particular care in cleaning any makeup around the edges.*

Maybe a facial skin peel? You know, we could always write in to 'This Morning', ITV. They love this kind of help, people with personal or facial … problems, well you know … what I mean.

The rain gets louder.

Aunty 5 *walks over to the window and watches the rain.*

I was in town one wet April. I had a bit of a chesty cough so I popped into Boots where my son worked. He treated me like a queen, sat me down, got me some cough mixture, cup of hot water and lemon then sent me on my way with a new brolly. It was from the latest range.

She turns to look at **Aunty 2**.

I'll leave it in the kitchen for you. It's raining hard, pointless going out now.

Aunty 5 *exits.*

Aunty 2 *takes a half-knitted scarf from the side of the sofa and starts to knit.*

Aunty 5 *re-enters reading from a pink piece of paper and holds two bottles of perfume.*

Aunty 5   Abusive husband brings home Indian bride illegally. Illegal wife finally runs away after her husband burns her. She is given two choices, shelter, but no money, just food parcels from the local church or a one-way ticket back home. There, that summarises your situation *and* that'll definitely grab the producer's attention. I've written it on some pretty pink paper. It should really capture people's hearts. May even help to reunite you with your sons.

Aunty 2   My sons live India, how they watch 'This Morning'?

Aunty 5   Oh, I'm sorry, I forgot. Well, you never know, stranger things have happened.

Aunty 5 *holds up the perfume bottles.*

Now, Elizabeth Arden's Green Tea Tropical or Yves Saint Laurent's Champagne?

Aunty 2   I not thirsty.

Aunty 5 *giggles then sprays the paper with some perfume and sniffs it.*

Mmm, perfect. I used to make my own paper. I was very good at art. I won something once. My son entered a silly drawing of mine for this competition in the local paper and I won! Oh, he was proud of me back then. I must have it somewhere. It's just a drawing of some flowers in a vase, very simple …

Aunty 5 *looks around.*

No, I didn't take it I … didn't have the time … time to take it. You leave in such a hurry don't you? Remember that woman last month? She only stayed for one night. I think she was Middle Eastern or something. You could tell she came from money or married it. Silk slippers, silk gown, she gave me a silk rose that fell off her slipper. Now, she came with a huge vanload of belongings, furniture, paintings, some beautiful throws. I offered to buy one off her, with that many you'd have thought … but no, she wasn't going to part with anything. I'm surprised she didn't bring the kitchen sink.

Beat.

Oh, I had a lovely view from my kitchen sink. We lived on top of a hill, under a huge tree, overlooking a picturesque valley, magical, like a fairy tale. Straight out of a novel. Brig o' Doon in Ayrshire. They call it Burns country because Robert Burns lived there once.

No response.

Robert Burns?

Beat.

The poet?

She recites a verse of Robert Burns's 'Tam O' Shanter'.

Ah, Tam! Ah, Tam! thou'll get thy fairin!
In hell, they'll roast thee like a herrin!
In vain thy Kate awaits thy comin!
Kate soon will be a woefu' woman!
Now, do thy speedy-utmost, Meg,
And win the key-stone o' the brig;
There, at them thou thy tail may toss,
A running stream they dare na cross.
But ere the keystane she could make,
The fient a tail she had to shake!

Aunty 2 *looks with a blank expression.*

Oh it doesn't matter. Do you know my husband never minded educating me? Don't you think that's rather strange? I thought the norm was to deny a woman knowledge? But no, not him. I joined a women's group. We read all sorts, classics, contemporary. On Thursday evenings my husband would dress me up like an Indian princess and insist I do poetry recitals for his well-to-do friends.

Beat.

Don't suppose you know any literature, poetry?

Aunty 2 *carries on knitting.*

Didn't think so, well I've plenty …

Aunty 2   I know English speech.

Aunty 5   *You* know an English speech?

Aunty 2   Yes.

Aunty 5   (*amused*) Well, let's hear this masterpiece.

Aunty 2 *clears her throat. She recites an extract from the* Shirley Valentine *stage play.*

Aunty 2   I'm staring out the window, tears trippin down me cheek. And in me head there's this voice that keeps saying, I used to be Shirley Valentine … what happened? Who turned me into this? Do you remember her *wall*? Remember Shirley Valentine? She got married to a boy called Jo and one day she came to live here. And even though her name was changed to Bradshaw she was still Shirley Valentine. For a while she still knew who she was.

Aunty 2 *finishes and stands proudly.* **Aunty 5** *laughs out.*

Aunty 5   Are you mad? That's what you call a speech? Talking to a wall? Whoever's taking your English class needs to take one herself.

Aunty 2   Why?

Aunty 5   Because that my dear is not a real speech.

Aunty 2   It speech from play.

Aunty 5   Sit yourself down and allow me to recite an extract from *Tess of the D'Urbervilles*.

Aunty 2 *sits.*

Almost at a leap Tess thus changed from simple girl to complex woman. Symbols of reflectiveness passed into her face, and a note of tragedy at times into her voice. Her eyes grew larger and more eloquent. She became what would have been called a fine creature, her aspect was fair and arresting, her soul that of a woman whom the turbulent experiences of the last year or two had quite failed to demoralise, but for the world's opinion those experiences would have been simply a liberal education.

Beat.

Sadly, you are still at Chapter One.

Aunty 2   That nice poem.

Aunty 5   It's not a poem. It's …

Aunty 2   I know poem.

Aunty 5   Really?

Aunty 2   Jasvir poem.

Aunty 5   Never heard of him.

Aunty 2   She read Punjabi poems for women on her radio programme.

Aunty 5   I'm all ears.

Aunty 2   Ears?

Aunty 5   The poem, let's hear it then.

Lights come up on HOUSE NO. 31. BEDROOM.

There is a double bed, single wardrobe and in the corner a very neat desk surrounded with white and coloured paper from A5 to A1, paints, pens and rows of recipes pinned up alongside a couple of drawings of Nigella Lawson's face (almost shrine-like). The bedroom door is also in view so you can see anyone enter the room.

The radio is playing in the background.

RADIO   Jasvir's Punjabi Radio programme. Jasvir recites one of her poems 'Dolli' ('Wedding Carriage') on the radio.

*Enter a beautifully dressed Asian bride (***Gurpreet***) and groom (***Raj***).*
They are wearing all the traditional garments worn at a Sikh wedding.
Their faces cannot be seen. They sit either side of the bed.

Aunty 2 *closes her eyes.*

Jasvir (*on the radio*) and **Aunty 2** recite 'Dholli' in Punjabi at
the same time.

Aunty 2/Jasvir   *Once you have been sent in the Dolli to your*
husband's house, do not leave the house until you die.
We will have peace of mind only if we could see your dead body carried
out from that house in a coffin.
Treat your mother-in-law as your own mother even if she does not allow
you to have food more than once a day.
Always respect her by bowing to her even if she beats you up and breaks
your bones.
Treat your father-in-law as your own father, even if he tries to touch you
with sexual desires.
Do not let anyone have even slightest idea about his behaviour, my daughter!
because that is how you will be faithful to them.
Treat your sister-in-law as your own sister even if she makes your life a
hell.
Even when your sister-in-law comes back from her own in-laws' house and
turns her brother (your husband) against you so to beat you up.
If you could not have a child because your husband is impotent, take the
blame yourself.
If you are not given enough food, do not let the whole world know about it
(keep quiet about it).
If you want your parents to live with dignity do not give others a chance to
lift a finger towards them even if your life has finished for you.
Once you have been sent in the Dolli to your husband's house do not leave
the house until you die.
We will have peace of mind only if we could see your dead body carried
out from that house in a coffin.

Aunty 5   Don't suppose you have the English translation?

Aunty 2 *reads from her textbook.*

Aunty 2   Once you have been sent in the Dolli to your husband's house, do not leave the house until you die.

We will have peace of mind only if we could see your dead body carried out from that house in a coffin.

Treat your mother-in-law as your own mother even if she does not allow you to have food more than once a day.

Always respect her by bowing to her even if she beats you up and breaks your bones.

Treat your father-in-law as your own father, even if he tries to touch you with sexual desires.

Do not let anyone have even slightest idea about his behaviour, my daughter! because that is how you will be faithful to them.

Treat your sister-in-law as your own sister even if she makes your life a hell.

Even when your sister-in-law comes back from her own in-laws' house and turns her brother (your husband) against you so to beat you up.

If you could not have a child because your husband is impotent, take the blame yourself.

If you are not given enough food, do not let the whole world know about it (keep quiet about it).

If you want your parents to live with dignity do not give others a chance to lift a finger towards them even if your life has finished for you.

Once you have been sent in the Dolli to your husband's house do not leave the house until you die.

We will have peace of mind only if we could see your dead body carried out from that house in a coffin.

Beat.

It much better in Punjabi.

Lights fade on the BEDROOM.

Aunty 5 (*to herself*)   That's rather tragic.

Aunty 2   See, I leaner English.

Aunty 5   Learning. It's Learn-ing. Dear, who takes your English class?

Aunty 2   They find someone take class from Poland.

Aunty 5   From Poland?

Aunty 2   Rhani said she cheaper than English girls. She speak English good.

Aunty 5   I should be taking the class! I should be taking the English classes! I could take you to the theatre. Oh, how wonderful would that be? Regular trips to Stratford-upon-Avon.

Aunty 5 *looks around the room excited.*

Where's the local paper? I don't think I've seen one being delivered for the past month.

Aunty 2   It in green carrier bag in kitchen.

Aunty 5 *exits, re-enters with a bag and shredded newspaper.*

Aunty 5   Is this it?

Aunty 2   I recycle. It help envirement.

Aunty 5   Next time, would you care to let us read it first?

Aunty 5 *shoves the shredded paper back into the bag and sits down. There is a sense of boredom and routine.*

What are you knitting?

Aunty 2   I knitting scarf.

Aunty 5 *(sighs)*   Oh.

Aunty 2 *glances over at* **Aunty 5** *then goes back to her knitting.*

Aunty 2   We nice day today. It nice when you can share. We share truth in here, why we here. I here start new life, fresh. I never thought I feel strong, but each day I stronger. Rhani say past is past. We must live in future. You tell me why you here?

No response.

Benji?

Beat.

Aunty 5   Why do you call everyone Benji!?!

Aunty 2   Because we are all sisters Benji.

Aunty 5   I hardly know you.

Aunty 2   You best friend with Benji who left. You not know her well.

Aunty 5   That was different. We connected instantly and she could speak English.

Aunty 2   I speak English.

Aunty 5   (*under breath*)   You manage to throw some words together.

Aunty 2   You trust to tell me things, I trust to tell you things.

Aunty 5   My journey's quite simple, nothing to tell.

Aunty 5 *exits.* **Aunty 2** *looks at her scar in the mirror, touches it and attempts to place some of her hair over it.*

She then goes over to the payphone and makes a call.

Aunty 2   Malik … I … I … learner English now and I …

She puts the phone down, stands for a moment then walks over to the dining table and writes in her homework textbook.

Aunty 2   Homework. My favourite recipe is homemade saag. In India I grew spinach in garden, pick leaf, wash dirt one. Chop …

Scene Two

BEDROOM Cont'd

Sat either side of the bed **Gurpreet** *turns and looks at* **Raj**. *She smiles and shyly looks away. A copy of Nigella Lawson's* How to be a Domestic Goddess *cookery book is lying on the bed.*

Raj   … and drain very well.

Ray *continues excitedly reciting an extract of Sausage and Spinach pie recipe from* How to be a Domestic Goddess. *He has memorised page 90 word perfect.*

Gurpreet, *still too shy to talk directly to* **Raj**, *speaks facing away.*

Gurpreet   Well Raj, I not know of this Nigella woman, but I am a good cook and once we …

Raj *interrupts by reciting Nigella Lawson's back-cover biography from* How to be a Domestic Goddess.

Beat.

I love Nigella Lawson's writing and I love her recipes.

Gurpreet   Then if you like this Nigella lady so much, I must learn to cook like …

Gurpreet *reads the title of the book.*

… a domestic goddess!

She giggles.

My mother said a bride must not talk too much on her wedding night, but your eyes make me want to tell you everything I am feeling right now. Dark brown like my papa's and your hands, strong like a real man …

She takes a deep breath, sits for a moment then starts taking her jewellery off. Bangles, earrings, nose ring, etc.

When I was a little girl, I said I would only settle for a man who loves me as much as my papa. Someone who talks to me with a gentle voice, laughs at my silly jokes …

She lifts her headscarf and smiles. She is nervous but in control. She unzips her top.

… Someone special. A lot of women dream of meeting someone special and I have and do you know what his name is?

She takes another deep breath, takes off her top, lies back on the bed and starts to gently lift her skirt then whispers

… Raj.

Raj *gets up and exits slamming the door.* **Gurpreet** *is startled.*

Scene Three

PARK BENCH

Aunty 4 *is sat staring out into space. Her hair is a mess. She is wearing a dirty white sari. On the bench are four stuffed carrier bags (pots, pans, clothes. One carrier bag is stuffed with carrier bags.) She holds against her chest a large Indian gold-framed picture (the picture is not revealed until later).*

Gurpreet *enters wearing her full wedding outfit. Her makeup smudged with tears. She looks around then sits next to* **Aunty 4**.

They sit for a while then **Aunty 4** *starts to rock and quietly mutter to herself.* **Gurpreet** *quickly stands and stares at her in horror.* **Aunty 4** *wanders off muttering to herself.* **Gurpreet** *watches her leave then stands around, awkward, then rushes off.*

Scene Four

Time passes

LIVING ROOM

Aunty 4 *is leaning against the door still wearing the dirty white sari and holding the four stuffed carrier bags. The picture is still being held against her chest.*

We hear a door open and close. **Aunty 4** *holds everything closer and starts to mutter. The words are unclear. She starts to panic, mutters louder. We hear voices then footsteps going upstairs. She collapses down, sits* *against the door and places the picture face down on to the floor. A blood-stained bandage falls out of one of the bags, she quickly stuffs it back in and puts her head in her hands. One hand is covered with a bloodied bandage. She collects her belongings and gently walks over to the massage chair.*

Time passes

It is dark. An unseen **Aunty 4** *is sat on the massage chair.*

Aunty 2 *and* **Aunty 5** *enter.* **Aunty 5** *is holding a torch and* **Aunty 2** *a chapatti pan.*

Aunty 2 *bumps into Joan's cutout.*

Aunty 5 (*heavy whisper*)   What was that!?!

Aunty 2   Joan!

Aunty 5 (*panicking*)   Shush.

They continue whispering.

Aunty 2   What we look for?

Aunty 5   Can you hear someone breathing?

Aunty 2   No.

A loud groan is heard.

I hear something now.

The groan quietens down. They hide, not knowing what to do.

Now it gone quiet.

Aunty 5   Oh gosh, my poor dear's returned. But, how did he know to end her life on her favourite chair?

Aunty 2   She dead. We hide!?!

Aunty 5   I'm sorry, I'm sure she's just resting, tired from wherever she's been …

Aunty 2 *now holds the torch in one hand and the chapatti pan in the other. She turns the torch towards the door then towards the curtain then towards the body on the chair.* **Aunty 5** *moves it away.*

Aunty 5   Please don't. What if she's not in one piece?

Aunty 2   You just say she alive?

Aunty 5   Yes, of course, I'm sorry, I'm being silly. I mean how else would she have got here?

Aunty 2 *quickly turns the torch towards* **Aunty 5***'s face.*

Aunty 2   He may be here in our house!?!

Aunty 5 *pulls her back down and takes the torch off her.*

Aunty 5   Don't be silly. Why return to the scene of the crime? Unless he wishes to be known for his crime? I mean we don't have an Asian Charles Manson?

Aunty 2   Who he?

Aunty 5   Famous killer who has a huge following of fans. More so apparently than Joan, which I simply refuse to believe. Only thing is they make their name by serial killing.

Aunty 2   Serial?

Aunty 5   Yes, they kill more than once and usually similar types to what they've already killed. Take Jack the Ripper for example: his bag was prostitutes, so …

Aunty 2   So he like to kill Asian women who leave their husband? But where he find more women?

Beat.

Aunty 5   Oh gosh, are you thinking what I'm thinking …?

Aunty 2   Fitiness first?

Aunty 5   Quick, press the alarm!

A loud snore is heard from the chair.

Aunty 2   She no dead. She sleeping!

Aunty 5   Asleep? My dear was only asleep. She must be starving. Please serve her favourite dish.

Aunty 2 *turns the living-room light on.*

The lamp, the main light's too bright.

Aunty 2 *turns the main light off and puts the lamp on and exits.*

Aunty 5 *hovers behind where* **Aunty 4** *is sat.*

I thought we were doing rather well, you, Joan *and* I. Didn't you? Well, I'm sure you wouldn't have had the strength to come back if it wasn't for Joan.

Beat.

You'll be pleased to hear that I've asked Rhani to invest in a stronger door. It's funny, but I always felt safe with you around. What I'm trying to say is, it's the people that make a safe house safe. Care for some of that nettle tea you're fond of?

Aunty 2 *enters with saag and places it on the table.*

Aunty 2   Fresh saag Benji.

Aunty 4 *wakes up muttering to herself in Hindi. The other* **Aunties** *see her face for the first time.*

Aunty 4   *Saag? Fresh saag?*

Aunty 5   She's not my dear … she's not …

Aunty 2 *calms* **Aunty 5** *down.*

Aunty 2   Benji please, she must be new Benji. She need us.

Beat.

Aunty 5   Of course. There are so many out there.

Aunty 4 *picks up the framed picture and holds it against herself then starts walking around.* **Aunty 2** *follows her around.*

Aunty 4   *My boys only eat fresh fresh saag.*

Aunty 2   *Benji?*

Aunty 5   Well, don't just follow her around, tell her where she is.

Aunty 2   *Benji, you are safe here. This is a women's refuge. You are safe here.*

Aunty 4 *is not responding.*

Aunty 5   What did you say to her?

Aunty 2   *Benji, he won't find you here.*

Aunty 4   *Baldev?*

Aunty 5   Who's Baldev?

Aunty 4 *walks over to the door and shouts up the stairs.*

Aunty 4   *Baldev? Baldev? It is time to get up.*

Aunty 5   I can't understand her. Is she okay?

Aunty 2   *Benji you are safe here.*

Aunty 5   Tell her she can have this Baldev locked up for what he's done to her.

Aunty 2   *Baldev won't find you here.*

Aunty 5   Well, what's she saying?

Aunty 2   *This is a safe house.*

Aunty 4   *No, no, no, this is my house!! My house!*

Aunty 5   Whatever you're saying is making things worse!

Aunty 4 *stops and looks at the wall.*

No, not there. That's where the clock goes. (*To* **Aunty 4**.) There is space over there.

Aunty 5 *points to an empty wall space.*

Aunty 2   *There is space over there Benji.*

Aunty 4 *calms down a little and walks over to the empty wall space.*

Aunty 4   *They will be home soon.*

Aunty 5   What is she saying?

Aunty 2   They home soon.

Aunty 2 *helps* **Aunty 4** *put the framed picture up. The picture is of an Indian man the same age as* **Aunty 4** *and two Indian boys in their late twenties.*

Aunty 4   *They will be home soon.*

Aunty 4 *starts to explore her surroundings, stops to pick up a slice of mango, smells it and smiles, then potters around tidying up.* **Aunty 2** *and* **Aunty 5** *look at the picture.*

Aunty 5   We cannot allow her to put images of men up.

Aunty 2   Why?

Aunty 5   It's the last thing she needs. Pictures of a family who have abused her. We all have our own way of dealing with things, but this, this … is completely wrong.

Aunty 2   She happy.

Aunty 4 *stops, slumps down on the massage chair and closes her eyes.*

Aunty 5   Is she? Look at the state of her. Such a worn-out face. I can tell she's lived a tragic life. I think we should get her out of that filthy sari and why wear a white sari on a day like this?

Aunty 2   White sari funeral.

Aunty 5   I know it's custom to wear a white sari to a funeral. Oh, a funeral eh? A peculiar moment to flee from home don't you think? Maybe she was never allowed out, kept hostage by a barbaric husband and as soon as she knew she was attending a funeral, she thought, this is my chance and fled! Or … or maybe she killed her husband, faked his death, funeral, but, then why run away?

Aunty 5 *takes one of* **Aunty 4**'s *carrier bags.*

Help me unpack her things.

They empty the contents, carrier bags.

Carrier bags? I prefer collecting shoes myself.

Aunty 5 *inspects* **Aunty 4***'s sari.*

Is that …?

Aunty 2   Blood.

Aunty 4 *mutters out loud.*

Aunty 4   No blood, no blood.

Aunty 2   *Benji, you all right?*

No reply.

Aunty 5   Oh the poor thing.

Aunty 2   She in shock. She talk in sleep.

Aunty 5   Oh.

Aunty 2   I take her nice park, Coombe Abbey tomorrow.

Aunty 5   Yes, fresh air should do her good.

Aunty 2   Today, she need me here.

Aunty 5   Could you bring me back some flowers? Any sort will do. I do so miss …

Aunty 2   She not know where she is.

Aunty 5   The smell of fresh flowers. I do so miss …

Aunty 2 (*to* **Aunty 4**)   *Benji, you must eat.*

Aunty 5   She needs a dose of female empowerment. I've got just the thing!

Aunty 2   She no need *Dynasty*, she need food.

Aunty 5 *exits on a mission.* **Aunty 2** *takes the plate of saag and chapatti, sits on an Indian stool next to* **Aunty 4***.* **Aunty 4** *opens her eyes.*

Aunty 2   I learner English Benji. This my saag. I make saag from my grandmother recipe. Everyone feel better after eat my saag.

Aunty 4 *smiles at* **Aunty 2***.* **Aunty 2** *then hand feeds* **Aunty 4***.*

Benji, it nice here. It very quiet but nice. I no scared here. There Lady Godiva in town centre on horse. She strong woman, like Indian women strong, but she need to put clothes on. I show you pound shop. They have pretty things for room. Room is small, but pound shop things make room nice.

Aunty 4 *coughs a little.* **Aunty 2** *puts the plate down and wipes* **Aunty 4***'s mouth with a tissue then takes some contents out of a plastic Tupperware container.*

See?

Aunty 2 *takes out a plastic statue of Lady Godiva.*

Lady Godiva on horse, shiny plastic and only one pound! She lived Coventry, many many years ago.

She then takes out two pink plastic jewellery boxes.

I have no jewellery, but this box, two for one pound! I like colour pink, I always wear pink when I was little girl. In here I put pen, pencil for English class. I only need one, you have other.

Aunty 4*'s clutched hand opens and on to the floor land a pair of gold wedding earrings.*

Oh, Benji, such pretty earrings!

She places them in the box.

There, for you.

Lastly she takes out a statue of 'The Kiss'.

Aunty 5 *re-enters holding a* Dynasty *box set. She watches* **Aunty 2** *with* **Aunty 4**.

This 'Kiss' stata…ue. English woman say, this good luck. I find boyfriend if I keep it. I tell them, we no need men to put smile on face, women look after women.

Aunty 4 *starts to fall asleep.* **Aunty 2** *puts 'The Kiss' on the table. While doing so a purse falls out, its contents of pound coins fall on to her lap.*

Aah, this money, I save and save then like Shirley Valentine I go Greece, sit on beach and look at the sea and no come back.

Aunty 2 *checks the time and walks over to the payphone, picks the phone up, puts money in and dials.* **Aunty 5**, *unseen, stands watching.*

Aunty 2 *speaks in a heated whispered Punjabi. We can barely hear her then she breaks into English, which is more audible.*

Aunty 2 (*on phone*)   *Malik, you will never hear from me again. I no longer fear you, but pity you.*

Aunty 2 *stops, takes a breath then speaks in English.*

And Malik I speak English now, see I can forgive you in English.

Aunty 4 *wakes.* **Aunty 2** *puts the phone down.*

Aunty 4   *Is this my home?*

Aunty 5 *disappears.* **Aunty 2** *helps* **Aunty 4** *up.*

Aunty 2   Yes, this nice home, this your home.

They exit.

Moments later **Aunty 5** *re-enters. She walks towards the curtain.*

Aunty 5   Can you see them Joan? His eyes, he's got his … his eyes, dark and so intense …

She rushes to the sofa with her handbag, pulls out an elegant hand mirror and puts some lipstick on. She stares at herself, and then with her finger she follows the lines on her face.

Reading my face, is like reading my palm, so many lines, showing all the different lives I have had to live. I never thought that this would be my life, living in one room with nothing but my thoughts. I'm intelligent, with some beauty, I'll find another … but who wants a second-hand woman? An animal in a zoo with no visitors? A damaged ballerina. Joan, do you know that there are far too many Tesses out there? Let's replace them, let's replace Tess with … Taj of the D'Urbervilles, John of the

D'Urbervilles. They've been harming innocent women for far too long … we women, also have needs, desires …

She prods the mirror with her finger.

When was the last time we were kissed? Touched? What is it with us? I desire to be caressed. I desire to feel like a woman …

She takes the mirror, holding it in one hand, with the other attempts to push her hair up. She giggles.

I'm going to show some flesh, flirt with the postman, make love in the back of a car. Do you know we are an object of desire? We're exotic, therefore hold a bit of … mystery.

Beat.

The women in this house simply don't understand me.

She looks at Joan.

You're right Joan, I should make them understand.

She continues doing her hair and makeup.

Scene Five

BEDROOM

Raj *is in bed. The radio is playing. An ironing board is out with a pile of shirts on it.*

RADIO   Jasvir's Punjabi Radio programme.

Jasvir is reciting 'Dolli' ('Wedding Carriage') in Punjabi.

Jasvir V/O   Thank you for listening. I will leave you again with my most requested poem, 'Dolli'.
Once you have been sent in the Dolli to your husband's house, do not leave the house until you die.
We will have peace of mind only if we could see your dead body carried out from that house in a coffin.

Treat your mother-in-law as your own mother even if she does not allow you to have food more than once a day.

Always respect her by bowing to her even if she beats you up and breaks your bones.

Treat your father-in-law as your own father, even if he tries to touch you with sexual desires.

Do not let anyone have even slightest idea about his behaviour, my daughter! because that is how you will be faithful to them.

Raj *throws his pillow at the radio. The radio starts to crackle.*
Gurpreet *rushes in.* **Raj** *starts to shout. What he is saying is unclear.*
Gurpreet *picks up the pillow and places it on the bed then turns the radio off.* **Raj** *quietens down.*

Gurpreet *slumps down on the side of the bed. She looks at* **Raj***.*

Gurpreet   *Treat your sister-in-law as your own sister even if she makes your life a hell.*

Even when your sister-in-law comes back from her own in-laws' house and turns her brother (your husband) against you so to beat you up.

If you could not have a child because your husband is impotent, take the blame yourself.

If you are not given enough food, do not let the whole world know about it (keep quiet about it).

If you want your parents to live with dignity do not give others a chance to lift a finger towards them even if your life has finished for you.

Raj*'s arm falls out. She looks at the arm, holds it for a moment then pushes it aside.*

Raj *wakes, grumbles and gets up, walks past her as if she is not there and exits. He shuts the bedroom door.* **Gurpreet** *gets up and starts ironing a shirt.*

We hear the bedroom door being locked. She rushes over to it and attempts to open the door. It is locked. She bangs the door. Female voices are heard outside. She backs off and goes back to her ironing.

She holds the shirt against herself, smelling it. On the wardrobe is a hanger with a pair of trousers. They hang as if they are in a standing position. She puts the shirt on another hanger which she places above the trousers then wraps a tie around the shirt. She almost has a complete man standing in front of her.

Raj, what did I say about stripy ties?

Beat.

I said my lovely husband does not suit stripy ties as his shoulders are too broad.

She takes off the stripy tie and replaces it with a spotty one.

Mmm … spotty only looks good on a man that smiles a lot and you my lovely are not one of them.

She takes the spotty one and replaces it with a dark chocolate one.

Aah, Raj, now you are looking very handsome. That was my papa's tie, his best tie, dark chocolate to match his dark brown eyes. My mother saved this tie for my husband.

Gurpreet *picks up the spotty and stripy ties and looks at them.*

Sadly, your mother has very poor taste in ties. If I could go to the shops I would choose many ties to suit you. You have dark features, so in the summer you can wear bright colours like mango yellow and papaya orange, maybe even lime green. Mother said choosing colour for clothes is much like choosing food, a feast for your eyes. In the winter you need to feel like the warmth of your home is with you outside. Darker colours like night blue, worn when two lovers walk hand in hand across the fields of …

SDFX   *Front door.*

Gurpreet *rushes around clearing up. She knocks the hangers with the clothes over. The bedroom door opens and* **Raj** *stands staring at her.*

Scene Six

LIVING ROOM

'The Kiss' statue is on the table. **Aunty 2** *enters wearing a coat, scarf and holds four plastic Tupperware containers with homemade curry and mango chutney.* **Aunty 4** *is sat on the massage chair in her nightie and her handbag is on her lap. Her coat is on the table.*

Aunty 2   Benji?

No response.

Benji, you remember what you tell me last month?

No response.

On your birthday your Baldev said …

Aunty 4 *turns and smiles.*

Aunty 4   I deserve a little day trip for being such a good wife.

Aunty 2   And you told me today is?

Aunty 4   My birthday.

Aunty 2   Today you are a queen. You must enjoy.

Aunty 4   Today my birthday?

Aunty 2   Yes Benji.

Aunty 4 *walks up to the picture and looks at it.*

Aunty 4 (*whispers*)   My Baldev said I deserve a little day trip for being such a good wife.

Aunty 4 *grabs her coat and puts it on.* **Aunty 2** *looks uncomfortably at* **Aunty 4**.

Aunty 4   Well?

Beat.

We must leave now … now!

Aunty 2   But Benji, you must change clothes first.

Aunty 4   Oh.

Aunty 4 *looks at herself.*

Is this my nightie?

Aunty 2   It new nightie for your birthday.

Aunty 4   It is my birthday?

Aunty 2   Yes Benji.

Aunty 4   Oh yes. Yes my birthday! I went on a day trip on my sister's birthday once. There was a new movie we just had to see.

Aunty 4 *exits. She speaks for the first time with joy.*

(*O.S.*) Oh, the excitement of getting off the bus, so many people, so crowded, we were used to our quiet village where everyone knew who you were and if you got lost someone would take you back home, but not here. The buildings towered over us like giants. We had to change our school clothes otherwise the police would have been suspicious …

Aunty 2   Sus…suspicious, that nice word. What it mean?

Aunty 4 (*O.S.*)   *When you don't trust someone or something.*

Aunty 2   Oh and then?

Aunty 4 (*O.S.*)   We went under a bridge to get changed.

Aunty 4 *re-enters wearing a (sari) petticoat and a matching blouse. She holds a bright sari. Across her chest is a fading red and blue bruise.*
Aunty 2 *helps* **Aunty 4** *put the sari on. This involves tucking one end of the sari into the petticoat, stretching the sari out and pleating the rest so it can also be tucked in. They stand either side of the room. Eventually they will meet in the middle. This is done during* **Aunty 4**'s *story.*

What we saw there will stay in my memory for ever. A group of young boys our age and younger. Some sleeping, some crying and some selling things to passer-bys. They smiled at us with such innocent eyes that I wanted to mother them. Then one boy ran up to me and asked me to play games with him. If we did, we would miss the movie. but how could we say no?

We walked with him to where he said we could play catch, but he had no ball. We turned to see some of the gang steals our clothes and bags. We stood there in shock. Such trusting eyes he had. In silence my sister and I walked away but the boy grabbed my hand and whispered in my ear, 'They make me, they make me.' I believed him, so, I took out the money we had saved for the movie and put it in his hand.

Aunty 2   Sad memory.

Aunty 4   No, fond memory.

The sari is complete. **Aunty 4** *stands smiling.*

He refused the money and followed me home. My parents took him in as they never had a son and he apologised every day for what he did.

Aunty 2   And …?

Aunty 4   And he never left my side … never … not until …

Aunty 2   Baldev?

Aunty 4   Yes my lost boy became my husband.

Aunty 2 *clocks the bruise on her chest.*

Aunty 2   Hye Benji … your …

Aunty 4 *throws the sari across her chest covering the mark.*

Aunty 4   My Baldev bought me this sari for my birthday. I put it on and we watched *Kabhi Kabhie* together. Our favourite movie.

Aunty 2   Benji, Baldev did he …

Aunty 4   He said I deserve a little day trip for being such a good wife.

Aunty 2   Benji, please …

Aunty 4   He said you pick nice place. But he was so tired after nightshift, so tired, he …

Aunty 2   He …?

Aunty 4 *turns to* **Aunty 2.**

Aunty 4   He …

Aunty 5 *enters wearing, over her Indian salwar kameez, a flash 1980's jacket with bigger shoulder pads than ever before. On her feet are blue killer high heels.* **Aunty 4** *gasps.*

Hye, your shoulders have swollen!

Aunty 5   I've had the original shoulder pads of Alexis's final episode inserted into my favourite jacket.

Beat.

eBay dears, eBay.

Aunty 5 *flashes her heels.*

And I found these beauties on the top of my wardrobe!

Aunty 2   You finally ready to leave house?

Aunty 5   With a little help from Joan anything's possible.

Aunty 4   *Your friend, I think she needs to see a specialist.*

Aunty 2   *She has been like this since I have known her. She does not know who she is.*

Aunty 5   It is very rude to … to start talking whilst I'm still talking.

SDFX   *Doorbell.*

Especially in a language another does not understand.

Aunty 2 *exits and re-enters holding a parcel.*

Aunty 2   Who is eBay?

Aunty 5   I'll take that, thank you.

Aunty 5 *takes the parcel off* **Aunty 2** *and relaxes on the massage chair.* **Aunty 4** *looks through her handbag.*

Aunty 4   Have we got sun cream?

Aunty 2   It raining Benji.

Aunty 4   But you can't sit on a beach without sun cream.

Aunty 2   I cooked lovely picnic for us.

Aunty 4   I'm sure you go through a jar of chutney a day.

They laugh.

Aunty 2   Day trips are so exciting.

Aunty 2/4   Seeing new places!

Aunty 4   Your English is improving.

Aunty 2   You help me, you speak good English to me.

Aunty 2 *starts to pack her containers into a travel bag.*

Aunty 5   Can you two keep it down? I'm trying to enjoy my massage, my ankles are swollen from practising Joan's walk in these heels.

Aunty 2 *laughs.*

What?

Aunty 2   You right, we respect elders. You rest feet.

Aunty 5   Are you questioning my age?

Aunty 2   You look …

Aunty 5   Incredible, I know. Anyway, why you both so dressed up?

Aunty 4   Baldev said I deserve a little day trip for being such a good wife.

Aunty 5 *sighs.*

Aunty 5   Oh yes, the day trip. It would have been rather nice to take in some sea air. I love it when the seaweed gets trapped between your toes. It's such a funny sensation but I just adore it. Sadly, not today. The trip's cancelled.

Aunty 2   The trip cancel?

Aunty 5   The driver's sick.

Aunty 4 *is confused.*

Anyway, it's bank holiday. Why would anybody want to spend the whole day with a bunch of old women … and me? They have their own families to spend time with, real families.

Aunty 4   What do you mean?

Aunty 2 (*to* **Aunty 5**)   You no heart?

This hits **Aunty 5***; she holds back any pain and hits back.*

Aunty 5   Yes a twenty-four-carat heart necklace. Tiffany's dear, Tiffany's.

Aunty 2   Why you steal from this Tiffany girl?

Aunty 4 (*to* **Aunty 2**)   What does she mean?

Aunty 5   I mean whilst we're all having to live in this … this … Well, if the truth be known, this shameful place for women.

Aunty 2   This real life. No *Dynasty*!

Aunty 4   Why is she insulting my home, why!?!

Aunty 2 (*to* **Aunty 5**)   This place save your life!

Aunty 4   Why!?!

Aunty 5   I wasn't insulting *your* home … I'm sorry, I didn't mean to upset you.

Aunty 2 *comforts* **Aunty 4**.

Aunty 2   Benji, you rest now. Baldev say you go on day trip, but we cannot go today, we go nother time.

Aunty 4   When?

Aunty 2   When … er …

Aunty 4   When another time? When?

Aunty 2 *looks helplessly at* **Aunty 4**.

Aunty 5   When it's not raining dear. Day trips are no fun in the rain are they?

Aunty 4   Well ... No.

Aunty 5   Everywhere looks nicer when the sun's shining. So why don't you pick somewhere and we'll arrange it.

Aunty 4   Yes, yes I will pick ...

Aunty 4 *mutters to herself.*

I will pick nice place.

Aunty 5   You do that dear.

Aunty 2 (*to* **Aunty 5**. *Whispers*)   Thank you.

Aunty 4 *starts to do her hair by the standing mirror.*

Aunty 2 *and* **Aunty 5** *watch her.*

I share something with you?

Aunty 5   Yes, of course.

Aunty 2   I saw ... Well I think I saw ...

Aunty 5   You think you saw what?

Aunty 2   Mark on her body.

Aunty 5   What kind of mark?

Aunty 2   Mark I think only man can make.

Aunty 5   Gosh ... and when you asked?

Aunty 2   She change subject.

Aunty 5   The classic change of subject, poor dear.

Aunty 2   I go collect food parcel, you please look after Benji while I out.

Aunty 2 *grabs her coat and goes to leave, but stands by the door and watches* **Aunty 5** *with* **Aunty 4**.

Aunty 5 (*to herself*)   Poor poor dear.

Aunty 4   Nice place. I pick nice place. Yes?

Aunty 5   Yes and you must choose a bright sunny day to match that bright sunny smile of yours.

Aunty 2 *smiles then exits.* **Aunty 4** *looks at her smile in the mirror.* **Aunty 5** *starts to open her eBay parcel.*

Aunty 4   Baldev said I have beautiful smile, like a film star.

Aunty 5   Well, he was right. But to keep that smile beautiful at your age takes more than toothpaste. You need to excite yourself, arouse those old bones of yours and what better way than a day of pampering and indulgence? So why don't you sit yourself down because …

Aunty 4 *turns and looks at* **Aunty 5**.

… In my goodie bag I have things that should transform you from Benjis to Barbies!

Scene Seven

BEDROOM

Gurpreet *is sat on the floor. She has a cut on her forehead. The ironing board has been knocked over and the pile of ironing is thrown all over the bed.* **Gurpreet** *picks up the chocolate-brown tie and holds it close to her.* **Raj** *enters ignoring her. He opens the wardrobe door then sits down at his desk. He starts to draw enthusiastically. The more intensely he sketches the more intensely he talks.*

Raj *recites an extract of Nigella Lawson's 'My Mother-in-Law's Madeira Cake' recipe from* How to be a Domestic Goddess. *He has memorised page 5 word perfect.*

Raj *stops and faces* **Gurpreet**. *He smiles awkwardly then produces a key from his pocket and offers it to* **Gurpreet**. *She takes the key and inspects it then walks to the wardrobe.*

Gurpreet   Where is my suitcase?

Raj *has gone back to drawing and is paying no attention to her. She puts her shoes and coat on and opens the bedroom door and exits.*

Raj *waits for her to leave then exits and returns with an old suitcase. He tucks the suitcase under the bed then goes back to his drawing.*

Scene Eight

PARK BENCH

Gurpreet *is sat with some paper and pen. She looks at the paper for a moment then writes.*

Gurpreet   Dear Mother, Uncle sent me here to be with someone special. A lot of women dream of being with this special someone and trust others to find them. Like I trusted Uncle, but Mother …

Gurpreet *stops for a moment then continues.*

Some dreams do not have a happy ending. Their special someone is …

She screws the letter up and shoves it in her coat pocket.

Oh, what is this, Gurpreet? What is this pity? You think Mother needs more pain in her life?

Gurpreet *looks up at the sky.*

Papa I hurt very badly and my … Raj he … I miss you Papa I miss you so much.

Aunty 2 *holding a food parcel walks by.* **Gurpreet** *quickly wipes her tears.* **Aunty 2** *takes a seat on the bench to catch her breath; a DVD drops out of her handbag.* **Gurpreet** *picks up the DVD.*

Gurpreet   Auntiji?

Aunty 2   Sorry, I miles away, thinking of this and that.

Gurpreet   *You cannot speak Punjabi?*

Aunty 2   All my life I only speak Punjabi, now I over sixty and learn English, I feel like new person, next I learn Greece.

Gurpreet   But … you are not English?

Aunty 2   Beti, I am Indian, I know, but why that change if I speak English?

Beat.

You are a new arrival?

Gurpreet *nods.*

Has husband taken you to see Lady Godiva?

Gurpreet *shakes her head.*

Coombe Abbey Park?

Gurpreet *shakes her head.*

Aah, still in honeymoon time?

Gurpreet *shakes her head, embarrassed.*

Gurpreet   I have a lot to do in the house but we will see everything one day. I must get back now.

Gurpreet *gets up then remembers the DVD.*

You dropped this.

Aunty 2   *Thelma and Louise*, very good friend movie.

Gurpreet (*defensively*)   My favourite movies are classic *Indian*, *Sholay* and *Mother India*.

Aunty 2   But you marry a boy from here?

Beat.

You are so young and you already learn to judge people?

Gurpreet *places the DVD on the bench.*

I seen it five time now, why you no borrow?

Gurpreet *shakes her head.*

Okay, no worry. I leave here for nother woman.

Aunty 2 *gets up and walks off.* **Gurpreet** *sits back down and reads the back of the DVD cover.*

Gurpreet   Thelma is married to a man who likes her to stay in the kitchen whilst he watches television. One day Thelma and her friend Louise decide to break out of their normal life. They jump in the car and drive off not knowing where to.

Gurpreet *smiles a little then walks off with the DVD in hand.*

Scene Nine

LIVING ROOM

On the dining table is a burning candle. On the floor is a jug of juice and some glasses, a tray of tea and a teapot. The teapot has a purple woolly tea cosy on it, which is in fact a legwarmer. **Aunty 4** *and* **Aunty 2** *are lying down.* **Aunty 2** *across the sofa and* **Aunty 4** *on the massage chair. They both have cucumber pieces on their eyes.*

Music   DOLPHIN NOISES.

Aunty 2   What that noise?

Aunty 4   I think it is what you call relaxing music. I bought some for my Baldev once and it give him nightmares. She is a very strange woman.

Aunty 2   She think she Joan Collin.

Aunty 4   Aah *Dynasty*. My favourite was *Golden Girls*.

Aunty 2   Yes, I Dorothy. Benji you be Rose, she very nice.

Aunty 4   That leaves us with …

Aunty 2   The slut.

Aunty 4 *and* **Aunty 2** *remove their cucumber pieces and giggle.*

Aunty 4   Hye Benji, your English is improving.

Just as they lie back and are about to place the cucumber pieces back **Aunty 5** *waltzes in wearing a tight green lycra cat suit with a matching* *towel placed around her neck and one purple legwarmer. The cat suit is stretched to its limit.* **Aunty 4** *bursts out laughing.*

Aunty 5 (*indicating* **Aunty 4**)   Oh, she's perked up.

Aunty 2 (*still giggling*)   You put smile on her face.

Aunty 5   Oh good.

Beat.

I haven't managed to get into this since my eating disorder. A bit of adjusting and here I am. Green Lizzy eat your heart out.

Aunty 4   You look …

Aunty 2   Green.

Aunty 5   My outfit isn't complete as I can't find my other legwarmer.

Aunty 2 *spots the teapot with the purple woolly tea cosy on it.* **Aunty 5** *does not and starts looking around the room for it.*

Aunty 2   What colour your legwarmer?

Aunty 5   Purple. Why? Have you seen it?

Aunty 2 *quickly removes the tea cosy and hides it.*

Aunty 2   No.

Beat.

Juice Benji?

Aunty 5   I'd love some.

Aunty 5 *reads from a small sachet containing sliced cucumbers.* **Aunty 2** *pours some juice for* **Aunty 4** *and* **Aunty 5***. She hands one to* **Aunty 4***.*

These apparently help with (*Reads.*) puffy eyes and dark circles. I've also got a face mask, kiwi and mango. It'll be like you've never left India with those fruits of the forest.

Aunty 2 *hands* **Aunty 5** *a glass of juice.*

Aunty 2   I have juiced mango, apples, carrots …

The **Aunties** *are about to take a sip.*

Coca-cola for fizz and chilli for spice.

They stop and put the drink down. **Aunty 5** *hands out some more cucumber pieces to* **Aunty 4** *and* **Aunty 2** *then places a towel on the floor, lies down and places the cucumber pieces on her eyes. They all lie back with cucumber pieces on.*

Aunty 5   I've some beauty tips for you ladies. Black eyeliner, out. False eyelashes, in. Lip liner and lip gloss is a must. I would suggest eye shadow, but having looked at your eyelids … may not give you the desired effect. Now, even at your age I still think it's best to wax the tash. That's the masculine side we don't want to reveal to all, don't you think? (*To* **Aunty 2**.) And dear, it took a bit of searching on the internet but I found a number for a top makeup artist for you. He's done all the big shows in West End London! I think he'll manage covering that scar up pretty well. He's not cheap though so you'll need to sell quite a few tinned Spams.

Aunty 2   What?

Aunty 5   Dear, I know you sell the contents of your food parcels. The church donate them to you, so you can do as you wish with them. I'm simply saying that you should up the price you're getting for them at the market. Then you'll be able to afford a gorgeous makeover with JJ. We need to call him. I'll have to do it. Your English is … let's just say you sound more Welsh.

Aunty 4   She can speak very good basic English.

Aunty 2   Teacher give me movie with strong women. She know Hindi movie give too many sad memory, she give me *Thelma and Louise*. Strong women.

Aunty 5: Really? Don't they jump off a cliff?

Beat.

Well, good for you. Now after this, we'll do some light exercise and later watch the saga of a wealthy Denver family in the oil business, Blake Carrington, the patriarch, Krystle, his former secretary and wife, his children, Adam, lost in childhood after a kidnapping, Fallon, pampered and spoiled Steven, openly gay, and Amanda, hidden from him by his ex-wife, the conniving Alexis. Most of the show features the conflict between two large corporations, Blake's Denver Carrington and Alexis's. Colby Co.

Beat.

I memorised that from the box set.

There is silence, which is soon broken when **Aunty 2***'s cucumber slides off. She attempts to pick it up; the other one slips off.*

Aunty 4 (*to* **Aunty 2**)   Slippery little things aren't they?

Aunty 2 *and* **Aunty 4** *laugh.*

Aunty 5 (*under breath*)   Bit like men.

Beat.

It's nice to hear laughter. It's a sign of healing. Dear, it shan't be long until you take that picture down hey?

Aunty 2   I made more saag, we eat with salad.

On hearing the word 'saag' **Aunty 4** *sits up.*

Aunty 4   *Fresh saag Benji. Please make fresh saag for my boys, my boys only eat fresh saag. You must please.*

Aunty 2   *Fresh saag is made Benji.*

Aunty 4   *They will be home soon. They will.*

Aunty 2   *There is plenty saag.*

Aunty 5   My Hindi has not improved in the last five minutes so I still cannot understand a word you're saying!

Aunty 2   Punjabi, I speak Punjabi.

Aunty 5   Well I don't!

Aunty 5 *turns off her relaxing music and exits.* **Aunty 4** *looks around.*

Aunty 4   My house?

Aunty 4 *looks up at the framed picture and smiles.*

My house.

Aunty 4 *sits back and starts to hum 'Kabhi Kabhie'.* **Aunty 2** *starts to knit. They both sit singing a couple of verses and the chorus.*

Aunty 5 *enters holding her* Dynasty *box set, she stands by the door and watches the Aunties happily singing away, she loses herself in the song then snaps out of it and cheerily waltzes in.*

Aunty 5   Ladies, I've sent the boys to their room.

Aunty 4   Oh, I didn't hear them come in.

Aunty 5   No, you never do. Anyway, we're going to have some fun so you can stop staring into space and join me for a night of adultery, high heels and high fashion. Yes this in my hand is the entire collection of *Dynasty*. A birthday gift for myself.

Aunty 4   But I wanted to watch a nice Indian film.

Aunty 5   Oh please, those films are all full of fantasy leading us to believe our lives would be the same.

Aunty 5's *bubbly mood changes.*

Now either sit and watch or leave me in peace.

Aunty 2   Don't you speak to Benji like that!

Aunty 5   Well, you're too soft with her. She has no idea who we are and where she is and we have a certain responsibility here. We should be telling her the truth, her truth.

Aunty 2   You not know her truth!

Aunty 2 *stares at* **Aunty 5**, *but backs down. She turns to* **Aunty 4**.

Benji, you take some tea to Baldev. It nearly time for him get up.

Aunty 2 *hands* **Aunty 4** *a cup of tea.*

Aunty 4   My Baldev, he is asleep?

Aunty 2   Yes, but he have nightshift soon.

Aunty 4   Oh yes.

Aunty 4 *mutters to herself.*

Boys, don't run around the house! Your father is trying to sleep. Benji, leave some dhal and two rotis for Baldev I don't want him to do nightshift on empty stomach.

Aunty 4 *walks over to* **Aunty 5** *and gives her a hard look.*

Baldev is sleeping. You must be quiet.

Aunty 4 *exits.* **Aunty 2** *starts to clear the table.*

Aunty 5   What are you doing dear?

Aunty 2   Tidy up.

Aunty 5   Everything? What about Baldev? Don't want him to be doing nightshift on an empty stomach now do we?

Aunty 2 *ignores her and carries on tidying up.*

I don't know how much more I can tolerate of her and her imaginary family.

Aunty 2   Why you no leave then?

Aunty 5   Sorry?

Aunty 2   Why you no leave? Benji, you not nice to her!

Aunty 5   Oh don't be ridiculous.

Beat.

I just don't understand why we are still pussyfooting around her?

Aunty 2   Pussy what?

Aunty 5   Someone give that woman a dictionary! Why are we keeping up with this pretence? She's not a child. Actually she looks old enough to be my mother.

Aunty 2   But I thought you eldest?

Aunty 5   How on earth can I be the eldest!?! Have either of you looked at yourself in the mirror lately? You jealous Krystle types, always gang up on the sophisticated and beautiful like Alexis. Krystle once said of her 'You either love her or hate her.' Much like myself.

Aunty 2   How many time I tell you she is in shock.

Aunty 5   Then arrange for her to see someone.

Aunty 2   They will lock up.

Aunty 5   Don't be silly.

Aunty 2   I look after her. I look after many Benjis.

Aunty 5   That is exactly what you're not doing, looking after her. She needs help, professional help. All we're doing is encouraging this madness. We'll all turn mad soon!

Aunty 2   Benji is my friend.

Aunty 5   Yes but she has problems beyond our control.

Aunty 2   She no have problem. You have problem! You no sleep! You never leave house!

Aunty 5   Me? Who's the crazy woman who's called her husband to forgive him!?! Isn't it enough having to wake every morning and see that scar? Isn't that enough for you to see sense!?!

Aunty 2   I told him that I feel sorry for him, that I am blessed and he is not. I am good woman. I not done wrong, then why I live with his pain?

Aunty 5   The bastard burnt you.

Aunty 2   I no scared now.

Aunty 5   Then why are you saving all your pennies to run away to Greece!?!

Aunty 2   I want nice life now. I have rid of my demons.

Aunty 5   The demon never leaves. What is wrong with you women? Open your eyes! You've forgiven him? Haven't you done well? You can't see your family or friends. Oh and look at the respect you've gained from your precious community. Where are they all!?! Women must look after women? Well, they've got a bloody funny way of showing it!

Aunty 4 *enters all flustered.*

Aunty 4   Is this my house?

Aunty 5   No.

Aunty 2 *rushes up to* **Aunty 4** *and comforts her.*

Aunty 2   Yes Benji. Now we go upstairs. I read you nice poem.

Aunty 4   My room is so small … I like it here …

Aunty 2   We go to my room. It has pretty view of garden. *Come.*

Aunty 4 *reluctantly exits with* **Aunty 2**.

Aunty 5 (*under breath*)   The demon never leaves you.

Aunty 5 *sits, rocking back and forth. She looks over to where the clock used to hang.*

Aunty 5   What time is it? I've a lot to do today, I've … When will she bring the clock back? Just because we don't do anything, doesn't mean we don't require the time.

She charges towards the curtain and lifts it.

He's still out there … his eyes staring at me …

The dove starts to coo. **Aunty 5** *rushes over to it and removes the emerald sheet revealing a beautiful green-winged dove flying around the cage.*

Oh you're flying. A sign from my dear absent friend.

She laughs out loud.

My dear must be alive. She's somewhere out there and she needs me.

Aunty 5 *turns to Joan.*

Joan, we're going out tomorrow and he will not stop me.

Scene Ten

BEDROOM

Gurpreet *is quietly putting some of her belongings into carrier bags. She looks exhausted. She takes a sip of water, her hands shaking. She spots a bit of blood on the* Domestic Goddess *book. She grabs the spotty tie and starts to wipe the book then takes the tie and wipes her forehead where the blood is dripping from. She then rests her head on the carrier bags and falls asleep.*

Moments later **Raj** *enters and grabs a drawing pad and pushes the chair towards Gurpreet and sits on it. He stares at her then starts to draw enthusiastically, looking up at her while drawing. The more intensely he sketches the more intensely he talks.*

Ray *recites an extract of the introduction of Nigella Lawson's* How to be a Domestic Goddess *cookery book. He has memorised the page word perfect.*

Scene Eleven

LIVING ROOM

Aunty 5 *stands in front of the standing mirror. She has finally transformed herself into Joan Collins. She no longer wears her Indian suit but a bright jacket with huge shoulder pads, a pencil skirt, frilly silk blouse and killer black heels. Her hair, however, remains the same, tied in a traditional bun. She looks the spitting image of Joan's cutout.*

She speaks with her Alexis accent.

The bird cage is on the table.

Aunty 5   'I've never had to pay for it Ashley, have you?'
'That's what closed doors are for, to keep out the curious.'
'I don't care if your relationship with Dex is personal
or professional, he is mine, in the boardroom and in the
bedroom.' Joan dear, would you care to see my Ms Collins
walk? I think you'll find it's ready to go.

Aunty 4 *enters staring at* **Aunty 5**. **Aunty 5** *carries on admiring her new image.* **Aunty 4** *carries on staring at her.*

Aunty 4   Who are you?

Aunty 5 *speaks without turning away from the mirror.*

Aunty 5   The name is Collins … Joan Collins.

INTERVAL

Act Two

Scene One

LIVING ROOM Cont'd

Music Dynasty *theme tune is quietly playing in the background.*

Aunty 4 *has in her hand some wrapped-up tissue paper and reads from a script.*

(They act out a scene from Dynasty *that* **Aunty 5** *has rewritten.)*

Aunty 5 *is stood in a dramatic pose, facing away from* **Aunty 4**. *She holds a fan in her hand and waves it.*

The room is draped full of clothes belonging to **Aunty 5**.

Aunty 4 *(reads)*   This script is in English and is presented as it was on American television …

Aunty 5   Dear, the dialogue.

Aunty 4   Dialogue?

Aunty 5   Yes.

Aunty 5 *walks over to* **Aunty 4** *and turns over the page and points.*

From there! I've spent a lot of time rewriting this scene. Continue until I say stop.

Aunty 5 *goes back to her posed position.*

Aunty 4   Chantelle, I'm busy …

Aunty 5   Oh for …

Aunty 5 *walks back over to* **Aunty 4** *and points at the script again.*

I'm Alexis! You're Krystle. Okay? And this is my high-class clothes boutique.

Aunty 4 *nods.* **Aunty 5** *goes back to her pose. She clears her throat.*

Chantelle, I'm busy with my new designs for …

Aunty 5 *turns to face* **Aunty 4.**

Oh, Krystle. It's you, here, in New York? What a surprise.

Aunty 4   I'm visiting Blake. He's here for business.

Aunty 5   Really, or are you secretly here to see my new designs? You could try something on? I'm branching out to plus-size women.

Aunty 4   Let's cut to the chase. Alexis, did you buy a gold bracelet of mine at the auction?

Aunty 5   Bracelet? Surely my dainty wrist wouldn't fit the same size as yours? Though now you mention it …

Aunty 4   I'd like it back. I'll pay you double what you paid for it.

Aunty 5   Still rather desperate aren't you?

Aunty 4   It's more than a bracelet to me. Blake gave it to me and asked me to wear it always to remind me of him.

Aunty 5   Oh, I was wondering why it had 'Krystle my love' engraved inside.

Aunty 4   And you still bought it?

Aunty 5   Oh please, I only noticed after I had purchased it. And realising that it was some poor woman's junk jewellery I gave it away.

Aunty 4   You gave it away!?!

Aunty 5   To my dog walker's daughter. She thought it was from the dollar store. Blake's taste never used to be so awful. It must have been a last-minute purchase.

Aunty 4   How dare you Alexis! You're not a woman, you're a heartless …

Aunty 5   Oh, I'm a woman in every way and Blake for sure had nothing to complain about, especially when we were alone. He used to cancel meetings away just so he could stay in bed with me all day long, but it now seems he can't seem to get away far enough from you Krystle, Denver to New York …

Beat.

You're supposed to slap me now?

Beat.

Well hurry and be gentle.

Aunty 4 *puts the script down, dropping the tissue on the floor.*

What have you dropped?

Aunty 4   I could not find a bracelet, but I have these earrings.

Aunty 5   I only *refer* to the bracelet. The point is she …

Aunty 5 *looks at* **Aunty 4***'s wedding earrings.*

Aunty 5   Oh dear. Please tell me you didn't wear these on your wedding day? Like wearing a pair of chandeliers.

Aunty 4 *is clearly upset by the comment.*

Don't look upset, I also had a traditional wedding. It was dreadful, simply dreadful! I bet Baldev chose them?

Aunty 5 *chucks the earrings on the sofa.*

We'll give them to charity. Right, where were we? The cat fight …

Aunty 4 *storms over to* **Aunty 5** *and slaps her hard.*

Ouch!

Aunty 4 *goes to hit her again, but* **Aunty 5** *grabs her arm then falls back on to the TV remote, which switches the TV on.*

What are you doing you crazy woman!?!

Aunty 4   You are wrong! You are wrong!

SDFX   *We hear an episode of* Dynasty *where Alexis and Krystle are fighting.*

A real cat fight breaks out between **Aunty 4** *and* **Aunty 5**. **Aunty 5** *tries to hold* **Aunty 4** *back, who has lost complete control.*

Aunty 5   What are you doing!?! Get off me!

Aunty 5 *throws the surrounding clothes at* **Aunty 4**. **Aunty 4** *pushes* **Aunty 5** *who then knocks Joan's cutout on to the floor.* **Aunty 5** *loses her balance and lands on top of it, breaking it in half.*

What have you done to Joan!?!

Aunty 4   You are wrong!

Aunty 4 *slowly walks up to the framed picture. She stares at it. Lost in a magical tale.*

Aunty 4   My wedding was the most beautiful of all weddings. Dressed like a princess, sweet and shy … my hands and feet hennaed with magical designs. Nervous and excited that my journey into womanhood had begun. Oh I did not want it to end, did I Baldev? But the ending was even more magical, fireworks that could be seen for miles. Even people from our nearby villages were there, celebrating with us. I was not marrying a stranger that day. I was marrying you Baldev … Baldev?

Aunty 4 *turns to* **Aunty 5**.

Where is my Baldev?

Aunty 5   There is no Baldev here! He does not belong here! This house, this house is a refuge. Do you hear me?

Aunty 4 *walks around emotionless.*

Aunty 4   This is not my home?

Aunty 5 *takes the picture down and hands it to* **Aunty 4**.

Aunty 5   This is no one's home!

Aunty 4 *puts the picture on the floor facing her.*

Aunty 4   I have no home! I have nothing! Nothing!

She slips off her sandals, lifts her sari and raises one leg.

Aunty 5   What are you …?

With all her energy **Aunty 4** *smashes the picture with her foot. There is some relief on* **Aunty 4**'s *face.*

Aunty 4 (*whispers*)   Nothing.

Aunty 2 *enters.*

Aunty 2   What have you done?

Aunty 2 *rushes over and leads* **Aunty 4** *away from* **Aunty 5** *and attends to* **Aunty 4**'s *foot.*

Aunty 5   She … she just …

Aunty 2   You hurt her?

Aunty 5   Please … I never meant to … I would never …

Aunty 2 *turns to* **Aunty 4**.

Aunty 2   *Benji, she won't bother you any more.*

Aunty 5   I didn't mean to … please let me help.

Aunty 2   You destroy this house!

Aunty 5 *stands helplessly for a moment.*

Leave!

Aunty 5 *puts on her heels, picks up two handbags, one gold and the other silver.*

Aunty 5   What do you think? Gold or silver with these? I'm rather taken with the silver.

Beat.

At least when I step outside, people can understand me. How have you managed to survive all this time without decent English?

Aunty 2   I learn now.

Aunty 5   You are learning. *Learn-ing!*

Aunty 2   How is your Hindi? Punjabi? Gujarati? Urdu?

Aunty 5 *looks at* **Aunty 2** *then at the bird cage.*

Aunty 5   It shouldn't be trapped in a cage.

She picks up the bird cage.

Unless it's a man.

Aunty 5 *hesitates then exits.*

Scene Two

Time passes.

PARK BENCH

Aunty 5 *is sat on the bench. She is still wearing her new outfit, only her hair is short and dyed black. On her lap is the bird cage. She closes her eyes and takes a deep breath.*

Gurpreet *enters holding the carrier bags from the previous scene. She looks lost, clocks the bench and sits next to* **Aunty 5**. **Aunty 5** *opens her eyes and gets up to leave.* **Gurpreet** *takes out a chapatti and starts to throw it at the birds.* **Aunty 5** *turns to* **Gurpreet**.

Aunty 5   Dear, I wouldn't encourage them. Here I am trying to release one and there you are trying to gather them around.

Gurpreet *continues to throw the chapatti.* **Aunty 5** *sits back down on the bench.*

You can't understand a word I'm saying can you? Pity, I have so many thoughts and no one to share them with. There was one but she left me. Chose the company of a beast over me. We just don't leave our husbands, no matter how badly they treat you. But I would never return.

Beat.

The day I left I saw a young English couple holding hands. They were going up the escalator and I was going down. As soon as I got to the bottom I felt short of breath, like my journey was coming to an end and before I knew it I was on their escalator. I followed them shop after shop. Is this what two people in love look like? Two birds flying around each other? Two mountains overlooking each other? I couldn't keep up, but I couldn't lose them. I needed to get close to this word *love*, so I looked it up in the dictionary but it only told me the meaning.

Gurpreet *seems to be listening*. **Aunty 5** *closes her eyes and takes another deep breath*.

Then I caught my reflection in a mirror. I saw a plain salwar kameez, long straight black hair and creamy skin. I looked closer, my kameez loose and baggy, so not to show off my body. My hair unkempt with even more grey hairs than my own mother. My skin heavy with dark circles and my eyes sore from crying myself to sleep. But the truly sad thing was, when I walked down the street, to me I looked no different from all the other women. Our women. The only difference was, I had set myself free and not realised. You silly woman, you are free. Like Joan Collins. Free to rule your dynasty. Free to conquer your demons.

Aunty 5 *looks at* **Gurpreet**.

You look like all the others. May I give you some words of wisdom? You see to be a strong independent woman, you must know the secret …

Gurpreet *looks back at* **Aunty 5**.

Give me your hand.

Aunty 5 *gestures hand*.

Hand.

Gurpreet *reaches out and* **Aunty 5** *takes her hand*.

The secret is …

Aunty 5 *places* **Gurpreet***'s hand on her shoulder*.

… shoulder pads.

Beat.

Please, give them a good squeeze.

Gurpreet *squeezes* **Aunty 5***'s shoulder pads. She is confused but does not let on that she did not understand this great secret.*

Gurpreet   Can I not be a simple woman with simple needs?

Aunty 5   Oh you speak English?

Gurpreet   To love her husband?

Aunty 5 *is a little embarrassed.*

Aunty 5   That is what we all wanted, but things change.

Gurpreet   I want my husband to look after me while I cook and clean for him, just like my mother did.

Aunty 5   Oh please, he can clean his own things.

Gurpreet   Women have a duty and I want to fulfil mine.

Aunty 5   Because you feel you have to?

Gurpreet   Because I enjoy being a woman.

Aunty 5   Then why label it as a duty!?!

Gurpreet   You pick on women like me, but look at you. You are not a real woman. A real woman is a good wife and mother. You choose short hair. You must speak your mother tongue, yet you choose to speak English. Are you not a strong woman with your own language? I am not afraid of being who I am. If my age cannot stay true, we will have no tradition left, just women trying to be man and woman at the same time!

Aunty 5   Don't you dare speak to me in that manner. Do you speak to your own mother like that?

Beat.

Well, do you!?!

Gurpreet *backs down.*

Gurpreet   No, never.

They sit in silence for a moment.

I am sorry … But … I have nothing if I cannot be a good wife to my husband.

Aunty 5   Your husband?

Gurpreet   My Raj.

Aunty 5   Your Raj is a good man?

Beat.

Gurpreet   Yes.

Aunty 5   Then why are you running away from him?

Gurpreet   I am not … I came out for walk.

Aunty 5 *picks up a carrier bag.*

Aunty 5   You've done the hard bit.

Gurpreet *grabs her bags and gets up.*

Gurpreet   They gave me a new life. They send money to my mother and how do I repay them? By leaving their son! I can't …

Aunty 5 *gently grabs her hand.*

Aunty 5   Wait, please … I'm sorry.

Aunty 5 *is emotional, but holds it in as much as she can.*

Please … please sit with me for a moment.

Gurpreet *takes a moment then sits on the edge.* **Aunty 5** *braves a smile.*

See over there.

Aunty 5 *points straight ahead.*

The house with the bright lights, number 23. Walk past and you will smell India. It's full of hope. It's full of women who look after women and when you're ready my dear, pay us a visit. There's always a room.

Pause. **Gurpreet** *looks at the dove.*

Gurpreet   You are releasing the dove?

Aunty 5   It's a pigeon dear. A green pigeon.

Gurpreet   No, it is an emerald dove, very rare. Some are found in India.

Aunty 5   Oh, I just thought …

Gurpreet   May I keep her?

Aunty 5   Well, I was told to release her the day I …

Aunty 5 *looks at the dove then at* **Gurpreet**.

Yes my dear, you may.

Aunty 5 *places the cage on* **Gurpreet***'s lap.*

Gurpreet   Thank you Auntiji.

Gurpreet *gets up.*

Aunty 5 (*almost sings the word*)   Auntiji? You call me Auntiji.

Gurpreet *exits.*

(*whispers*) Auntiji.

Scene Three

LIVING ROOM

Aunty 4 *and* **Aunty 2** *are sat on the sofa.* **Aunty 4** *is wearing her birthday sari, wedding earrings and a bandage on her foot.*

TV   Kabhi Kabhie *the iconic Indian movie. The* **Aunties** *are humming along to the song.*

Music   'Kabhi Kabhie'.

Aunty 2   Benji, you be okay? I have English class, but I stay if you need me?

Aunty 4   Please, you go.

Aunty 2   I in computer room. You get me if you need anything.

Aunty 4   I am okay now. I will finish watching movie.

Aunty 2 *exits.*

Aunty 4 *gently starts to sing along to 'Kabhi Kabhie'*

After she has sung a verse she gets up and starts dancing to the music as if dancing with her husband.

Aunty 4   Baldev, tell me again the time you raced the bull and won?

Beat.

But they are so fast, how did you do it?

Laughs, almost childlike.

This is a perfect birthday. Oh, where are you taking me? On a day trip for being such a good wife? But, Baldev … you look so tired, so tired. We go another time. Oh, you have a special surprise planned with our boys, then who am I to refuse?

She looks away, almost movie-like.

Sometimes I have to pinch myself to see how lucky I am. I am still so shy around you. My heart is beating so fast.

She giggles. **Aunty 5** *enters and watches* **Aunty 4**. *Unseen.*

As **Aunty 4** *dances lights come up on the BEDROOM.*

Gurpreet *is dancing with the bird cage.* **Aunty 4** *and* **Gurpreet** *both giggle as they dance faster and faster.*

Aunty 4 *stops as her foot is in pain.* **Aunty 5** *rushes over and helps her sit on the massage chair.*

The lights fade on the LIVING ROOM.

BEDROOM

Gurpreet *is still dancing. She slips. The cage lands on* **Raj**'s *shrine, knocking a glass with a little paint water.*

Gurpreet *is in a complete fluster.*

Gurpreet   Oh no …

Gurpreet *turns to the door.* **Raj** *is standing there.*

Gurpreet *rushes towards him. He pushes past her and shuts the door on her. He places a chair so the door cannot be opened. He sits on the bed and places the duvet over his entire body. He starts to rock while under the duvet.*

Gurpreet knocks on the bedroom door. **Raj** *does not answer. She knocks louder then stops.* **Raj** *carries on rocking.*

Raj? Raj …?

Gurpreet *sighs and leans against the door.*

Raj, open the door. I am sorry.

She sits down, waits for a reply then speaks again.

If you let me back in I will buy you your favourite chicken burger. If you don't let me in I will eat it all myself. You don't want me to eat it all myself do you?

No answer.

Raj, you are going to have to open the door soon.

Beat.

Raj, please. No one is home. It will be just you and me if you let me in.

Raj *slowly takes the blanket off and stares at the door.*

Raj. I will count to ten then you must let me in. One, two, three, four …

Raj *walks towards the door. He has an awkward walk. He is about to open the door but doesn't.* **Gurpreet** *stands up.*

I can hear your heavy feet on the floor. Now hurry … five, six, seven, eight. I am only counting to ten Raj, nine, nine and a half, nearly there Raj … ten!

Raj *picks up the chair instead and throws it at the door.*

Raj …!?!

Gurpreet *bursts in.* **Raj** *has worked himself up. He is out of control. He paces up and down.*

Raj please … stop this … please … Raj …

Raj *stops and stares at* **Gurpreet**.

Raj, you're scaring me …

Raj *starts to lash out with his arms at nothing but the air then starts to hit himself. He is now crying loudly and pointing to a drawing.* **Gurpreet** *does not understand. She just stands watching.* **Raj** *rushes to the damaged drawing and starts to rip it up.*

Please stop, please … I didn't mean to ruin your work!

She tries to reach out to **Raj**, *trying to stop him hurting himself.*

Raj, you're hurting yourself! Your mother and sister will be very upset with me … please.

Gurpreet *lets him go and shouts right in his face.*

Just listen for once!!

She finds the strength and grabs **Raj**, *who is bigger than her, and holds him tightly.*

They can't see you upset. They must not see you upset!

Raj *manages to release himself and carries on lashing out at himself. They struggle. She continues trying to stop him from hurting himself. After a while she stops trying.* **Raj** *eventually crashes on to the floor shaking and crying.*

Gurpreet *stands watching until he has no more energy to carry on. She eventually sits herself down next to him.* **Raj** *naturally collapses into her lap like a child. She rocks him to sleep, trying very hard to hold back her own tears, but fails.*

We hear a front door open and slam shut. She rushes out of the bedroom. **Raj** *is still curled up on the floor.*

OFF STAGE: We hear a **Woman** *raising her voice and* **Gurpreet** *trying to quieten her.*

Woman *(O.S.)   Where have you been? Where have you been!?! Leaving your husband to feed himself! What kind of wife are you!?!*

Gurpreet *(O.S.)   Sorry! I am sorry! Please! No, No please …!*

We hear a loud scream.

Gurpreet *enters the bedroom with a bleeding mouth. She grabs the brown tie and wipes her lip with it. She looks at Raj on the floor and places the blanket over him then exits.*

Gurpreet *(O.S.)   Don't you dare touch me again or I am calling the police!*

OFF STAGE: **Gurpreet** *is heard being beaten, then there is a moment of silence before she re-enters, crawling along the floor towards the bed. She is beaten badly. She cannot get on to the bed. She lies on the floor instead.*

Scene Four

LIVING ROOM Cont'd.

Aunty 4 *is sat on the massage chair with a balti dish of water in front of her.* **Aunty 5** *is sat on a stool next to her with a towel and some bandages.*

Aunty 5   Dear, you really shouldn't be dancing with an injured foot.

Aunty 5 *spots a tiny piece of glass in* **Aunty 4**'s *foot.*

I'm sorry this may hurt, it's just a bit of glass.

Aunty 5 *gently takes the piece out.* **Aunty 4** *does not react.*

Self-harm is, well it's just not …

Aunty 5 *places* **Aunty 4**'s *foot in the balti dish.* **Aunty 4** *winces but allows* **Aunty 5** *to wash her foot.*

Dear, what we all need is something to release our frustration. I would suggest a glass of fine wine but I'm not sure if you have a taste for it. Dancing and fine wine, now that was something my husband used to be an expert in. Dining in, dining out.

Aunty 4   Who are you?

Aunty 5 *continues with her tale.*

Aunty 5   Every time we had guests for dinner my husband would belt out his favourite Scottish folk song …

Aunty 5 *starts to sing 'The Women Folk', a traditional Scottish folk song. Mocking her husband.*

O sarely may I rue the day
I fancied first the womenkind;
For aye sinsyne I ne'er can hae
Ae quiet thought or peace o' mind!
They hae plagued my heart, an' pleased my e'e,
An' teased an' flatter'd me at will,
But aye, for a' their witchery,
The pawky things I lo'e them still.

Aunty 5 *loses herself in the chorus. She gets up and starts to twirl as if she is performing once more in front of a room full of guests.*

O, the women folk! O, the women folk!
But they hae been the wreck o' me;
O, weary fa' the women folk,
For they winna let a body be!

Aunty 4   Who are you?

Aunty 5   Our guests loved it, loved him, me? I could enjoy it to a point then I would rush to my room and make a mark on my body, reminding me that I still have some control over what I do.

Aunty 4   Who are you?

Aunty 5   I don't know, okay!

Beat.

I'm sorry.

Beat.

You should rest.

Aunty 5 *picks up the picture.* **Aunty 4** *grabs* **Aunty 5***'s hand.*

I will clean it and bring it back.

Aunty 4 *stares at* **Aunty 5**.

I promise.

Aunty 4 *releases her hand.* **Aunty 5** *exits.*

Aunty 4 *starts to shout.* **Aunty 5** *rushes in still holding the picture, puts it down and rushes to her.* **Aunty 4***'s hands start to shake.* **Aunty 5** *tries her best to stop them.*

Your hands … they're shaking. Your hands dear …

Aunty 5 *tries her best to comfort her. She rubs her hands.*

There, there dear.

Aunty 4 *struggles to breathe.*

Dear … you must keep breathing.

Aunty 5 *helps by taking deep breaths with her. She manages to control her breathing with* **Aunty 5***'s help.* **Aunty 4** *starts to tug at her sari.*

What is it dear?

She carries on tugging.

Is it too tight?

Aunty 4 *nods.* **Aunty 5** *loosens her sari. She then fetches a glass of water and gives it to* **Aunty 4***; her hands are still shaking.* **Aunty 5** *holds the glass and* **Aunty 4** *drinks from it.*

Almost zombie-like she speaks out.

Aunty 4   How a mother survive? Nothing … nothing to mother. Nothing …

Aunty 5   Dear, he tried to kill you.

Aunty 4   I killed him.

Aunty 5   What?

Aunty 4   I killed my Baldev and my boys.

Beat.

Aunty 4   I killed my Baldev and my boys.

Aunty 5   He must have been an evil man and the boys …

Aunty 4   No! No! No!

Aunty 5   Please, you're not alone. I too have …

Aunty 4   Baldev said it my birthday! We go on day trip for being such a good … good … So tired … he was so tired. He could not see with tired eyes. He did not … could not see … the van … the … van … Baldev in car … in car …

Aunty 5   Car *accident?*

Aunty 4 *nods.*

Aunty 4   Baldev was so tired, nightshift then straight to day trip. My day trip for being such a good wife. He was so tired, he did not see …

Aunty 5   The van?

Aunty 4 *nods.*

Aunty 5   And your boys?

Aunty 4 *looks away.*

Aunty 5   Only you survived?

Aunty 4 *puts her head back and closes her eyes.*

Aunty 5 *looks at her for a moment then gets up and puts the picture back on the wall. She stares at it.*

If the truth is something that is so tragic that you wake up feeling the pain of loss every day, I would choose to believe the lie.

She walks towards the curtain.

What if you've left the demon, but the demon won't leave you?

Aunty 2 *enters and looks at a peaceful* **Aunty 4** *then at* **Aunty 5**, *who turns to face her.* **Aunty 5** *looks on helplessly.*

Aunty 5   I have nowhere else to go.

Beat.

Aunty 2   You cut hair?

Aunty 5   My hair?

Aunty 5 *touches her hair.*

Oh … yes I cut my hair.

Aunty 2   You think you Joan now?

No response.

How she help you? Huh? How?

They stand looking at each other. **Aunty 5** *trembles as she speaks.*

Aunty 5   Well … she is … a woman of … of great … er … integrity, no, I mean … power. And power is … what I mean is if there were more women with power … we'd …

Aunty 2   I take Benji upstairs.

Aunty 5   Wait … please. I would like to comb her hair. It doesn't look like it has been combed for weeks.

Aunty 2 *gives* **Aunty 5** *a hard look.*

Aunty 2   Why?

Beat.

Aunty 5   Because women must look after women.

Beat.

I'll be there for her. From now on I'll be there …

Aunty 2   Benji no longer need look after. She leave in morning.

Aunty 5   Leave? Why?

Aunty 2   Her daughter-in-law have baby. She grandmother now. After her family funeral she run away. She not remember anything, She in shock, then police find her and they bring Benji here. She no need refuge. She need to go home.

Aunty 2 *gently wakes* **Aunty 4** *and exits with her.*

Aunty 5 *looks at the cutout on the floor, picks up Joan's face and looks her straight in the eyes.*

Aunty 5   You cannot help anyone. See? Another one gone!

She drops Joan and charges over to the curtain and lifts it up.

And he … he is still out there Joan!

Aunty 5 *pulls the curtain down.*

Take a good look!

She pulls the other curtain and nets down, revealing the inside world to the outside world.

Take a good look at the damaged ballerinas!

Scene Five

BEDROOM

Gurpreet *is asleep in bed.*

Raj *enters holding a bunch of flowers and a packet of lollipops. He is in his underwear and a pair of mismatching socks. Round his neck is his chocolate-brown tie (loose). His hair is a mess.*

He takes the hot-water bottle from off the bed and pours the contents of water from it into his paint glass. He fills the glass up with too much water. It overspills. He stops and looks at the water overspilling and giggles. Then takes the glass over to the bed and puts it on the floor and shoves the flowers into the glass, walks back over to the desk, takes off his tie and starts to wipe the water.

The water continues spilling off the desk. He presses the tie harder. He starts to work himself up then steps back, knocking the glass with the flowers on to the floor. He grabs all but one flower that is left on the floor and shoves them inside the wardrobe. He then sits on the edge of the bed staring into space.

Raj *sits for a while and eventually* **Gurpreet** *wakes up.* **Raj** *is still sat on the edge of the bed staring into space.*

Gurpreet   Please can I have some water, Raj?

No reply.

Raj, I need to take my medicine.

Gurpreet *reaches for a glass. It slips off the table and lands on the floor.* **Raj** *does not react. The dove starts to flap around in the cage.* **Raj** *gets up, takes some bird food off the side and feeds the dove.*

You know how to feed a bird when it is hungry, but not your wife when she is thirsty. What sort of a man are you Raj!?!

The dove quietens down and **Raj** *sits back down in exactly the same spot as before.* **Gurpreet** *attempts to get out of bed, but fails; the pain is too much.*

Please Raj … how can you just watch?

She lies back staring at the ceiling.

Your mother told my uncle that she had a beautiful and intelligent son and I was so happy.

She turns to face **Raj***. He is staring out into nothing.*

Do you remember the long day I wore a red sari? That was our special day to bring us together. I sent my mother photos and I wrote a letter with such lies, such lies I wrote to my own mother. I told her that day was the happiest day of my life, because, Raj, that day is supposed to be the happiest day of a woman's life …

Raj *is silent.*

I know you know things. They whisper then tell me to do things. If I say no, they send you upstairs and lock your door, but I know you can still hear. You can hear your mother and your sister shouting at me. Hear me crying. One time, they forgot to lock your door and you watched from the stairs. Your sister pulled me by my hair to the kitchen, your mother was standing by the cooker. I did not make enough rotis so your mother put my hand on the hot cooker. I screamed, but she would not stop, but pressed my hand harder and harder. I pushed her away and your sister hit me with the hot pan. I screamed like a child. She hit me again to stop my screaming. I ran to you, but you did nothing, just let me give you your dinner. You did not ask why my face and hand were red, you did not say anything! You never say anything … my Raj … my husband.

Gurpreet *is shaking.*

The truth is, Raj, you are not my husband and I am not your wife.

She attempts to get out of bed again, but falls on the floor. She manages to put her hands together in a prayer position.

Please forgive anything I may have done to deserve this pain. Please forgive me and take this pain away, as I have not much strength left … please.

She takes a deep breath, picks up the glass off the floor and pours herself a glass of water. She then takes a pill and swallows it. She goes to take another pill but **Raj** *snatches the pill off her. She tries to take the pill off him but he won't give it to her.*

Stop being silly and give me my tablet! Raj! Raj, you must listen to me. You must! I am hurting. Give it back!

No reply. She tries again.

(*Gently*) Raj …

Raj *responds to her gentle approach. He stares at her.*

My dear Raj please …

Raj *kneels down in front of her. He examines her face as if looking for something.*

Please give Gurpreet her tablet.

Raj *gently grabs* **Gurpreet***'s tongue as she speaks. She pulls away.*

Raj, stop being silly…

Raj *tries to grab her tongue again.* **Gurpreet** *stops and looks at* **Raj***. His hand is in position ready to have another go. She looks for a moment. Then slowly speaks, leaving the tongue out.*

Raj …

Raj *takes her tongue and places the pill on it then takes the water and holds the glass so she can drink from it.* **Raj** *then puts the glass down and goes and sits back on the edge of the bed in exactly the same position as before and continues staring into space.* **Gurpreet** *looks at him.*

Thank you Raj.

Gurpreet *spots the single flower and picks it up then looks at* **Raj***.*

Thank you.

Scene Six

LIVING ROOM Cont'd

Aunty 5 *is now sat curled up on the sofa staring at her ballerina box. The ballerina slowly going around and playing an old tune.*

Aunty 5   Yes, sadly my wedding was of the traditional sort. Crowds of strangers staring at me, like a circus act. My face painted with a smile, much like a clown's face, hiding behind a mask. Heavy makeup, heavy jewellery, heavy heart. I'm sure no one even saw my face … except the one I married, he saw. He saw the terror in my eyes.

She takes a kameez (Indian top) that is hanging to dry and puts it on. Standing in her English skirt and Indian top she stares at herself in the mirror, hard, then quickly takes all her clothes off until she is in her underwear and continues staring.

Who am I?

Aunty 2 *enters, looks at an exposed* **Aunty 5**. *She grabs a thick Indian scarf and rushes over to* **Aunty 5** *and covers her up then holds her tightly.*

Auntiji. Ji in auntiji means respect and this girl called me Aunti-*ji* with such tenderness.

Aunty 5 *looks helplessly at* **Aunty 4**.

What has become of this auntiji?

Aunty 2 *guides her to the sofa. They sit down.*

I did not grow up with a single auntiji, but an uncleji … Taj, or he *said* he was an uncle because if he didn't I would not let him …

Aunty 2 *gently strokes* **Aunty 5***'s hair.*

Aunty 2   I here for you, Benji. I here.

Aunty 5   At fifteen I married my uncle Taj.

Aunty 2   Why marry?

Aunty 5   I was carrying his child. I was carrying the child of a man twice my age and twice my weight and he crushed me with both.

Aunty 2   Where your child?

Aunty 5   Should a child not be told the truth?

Aunty 2   Benji, where your child?

Aunty 5   I can see him … I can see his eyes …

Aunty 2   Benji?

Aunty 5   My son is with my husband and there's nothing I can do. You see, you cannot accuse your husband of such a thing, but I wanted my son to know the truth … that I was taken by his father, but the thing is my husband knew I would tell my son my truth one day. So he planted the seeds and watched as my son spat in my face and called me a whore. Saying father already told him, women my age only marry older men for their money. That I'd been sleeping around for years and now that I'd taken every penny I was ready to move on.

Aunty 2   Oh Benji.

Aunty 5   I remember my son's eyes, his eyes staring at me, then it went silent and out of nowhere, my son punched me in the jaw.

Aunty 5 *can no longer hold the pain in. She releases a painful cry, almost a howl.*

I want it to leave me … this pain … this feeling inside … it won't leave me. Make it leave me!

Aunty 5 *grabs the statue of 'The Kiss' and throws it at the window. The window smashes.*

She looks out for a moment.

I can't see … I can't see his eyes any more.

Aunty 2 *places* **Aunty 5***'s face in her hands and gives her a loving stare.*

Aunty 2   Your demon has left you.

Aunty 2 *holds* **Aunty 5.**

Scene Seven

BEDROOM. It is dark.

Gurpreet *is asleep in bed.*

Raj *enters and stands on the chair. He starts to talk with great enthusiasm.*

Raj *recites an extract of the introduction to Nigella Lawson's* How to be a Domestic Goddess *cookery book. He has memorised the page word perfect.*

Gurpreet *wakes on hearing his voice. She is fully dressed in an Indian suit which she has fallen asleep in.*

Raj *runs to the bedroom light and turns it on revealing the bedroom walls. They are covered with drawings and paintings of* **Gurpreet** *and her journey. Captured moments that* **Raj** *has seen, but could never put into words. Their wedding day. His mother slapping* **Gurpreet**, *her crying by the side of the bed, her feeding him. Behind* **Gurpreet** *is her face stuck on the wall. Each piece of paper has different parts of* **Gurpreet**'s *face. The picture is of* **Gurpreet** *as a goddess.*

Gurpreet   Oh Raj.

Raj *rips out some paper and starts to stick it up above* **Gurpreet**'s *face.*

Raj *finishes. It reads in big letters 'Domestic Goddess'.* **Gurpreet** *is overwhelmed.*

Raj *rushes out of the bedroom.* **Gurpreet** *looks at all the pictures.*

Raj *re-enters holding a small saucepan with a plastic spoon.*

For me?

Raj *nods.*

Remember what I do? Hold the handle with both hands.

Raj *carefully walks towards* **Gurpreet**.

Mmm, let me guess. Is it tomato soup with your special surprise of pepper, chilli sauce and aubergine chutney?

Gurpreet *smiles.* **Raj** *feeds her a spoonful. She starts to cough.* **Raj** *drops the spoon.*

No Raj, the soup is lovely, it is just hot, *hot*, and my mouth is … is a little sore.

Gurpreet *starts to blow on the soup.* **Raj** *joins in. They both sit blowing on the soup. Then* **Raj** *takes a sip himself before giving* **Gurpreet** *another go.*

Mmm that's nice.

Raj *carries on feeding her; after a couple more spoons, she stops and starts to cry.* **Raj** *quickly puts the plate down.*

Raj, they are not tears of sadness.

Gurpreet *giggles.* **Raj** *copies. They both giggle.* **Gurpreet** *suddenly stops as she is in pain.*

The hurt will go soon Raj.

Raj *jumps on to the bed giggling and pointing at the wardrobe.*

I still don't know what you want me to do?

Gurpreet *opens the wardrobe door. She takes out her suitcase which is packed. She turns to* **Raj**.

Gurpreet   Who did this?

Beat.

Am I going somewhere?

Raj *takes the suitcase and places it in her hand.*

Even you know I don't belong here?

Gurpreet *looks on smiling. She places the suitcase down.* **Raj** *grabs her coat and helps her put it on. She then walks over to the bird cage.*

When was the last time you saw a blue sky?

She takes the bird cage and suitcase and goes to leave. She looks back and **Raj** *is waving at her. With a tear in her eye she exits.*

Scene Eight

LIVING ROOM

Music   *Traditional Greek folk music.*

Twister game is placed on the floor. **Aunty 5** *and* **Aunty 2** *are entangled in some awkward positions.*

Aunty 5   I can't breathe down here, hurry up and make your move!

Aunty 2   I say you do yogi Benji, like me, then you not be so stiff!

Aunty 5   Whose Jane Fonda workout inspired you in the first place? No … no … can't hold on any longer.

They both collapse on to the mat laughing.

The doorbell rings.

Aunty 2 *runs around tidying up while* **Aunty 5** *composes herself.*

Aunty 2   Rhani say new girl coming today. She is early, house not tidy.

Aunty 5 *exits and re-enters followed by* **Gurpreet** *holding her suitcase and bird cage.*

It is you?

Gurpreet   Were you expecting me?

The **Aunties** *look at each other, unsure.*

Aunty 5   Would you like a cup of tea or coffee? I've started baking so if you fancy millionaire shortbread? Plenty left.

Aunty 2   Benji is silly. She think biscuit will make her rich.

Aunty 5   I was once and I do know how to accumulate wealth. Once I'm on my rather pretty feet again I'll become a lady of leisure once more.

Aunty 2   I go to leisure centre, so I am a lady of leisure.

Aunty 5   You still do say the …

Gurpreet *starts to giggle. The* **Aunties** *look at her, puzzled.*

Do we amuse you?

Gurpreet *nods her head, still giggling.*

Gurpreet   When we were in India my uncle found English man's video tape. They had very good recording of a black-and-white film with a double act; you have their ways.

Aunty 5   Ah, it must have been a young Sophia Loren film. I've often been told I have a little Sophia about me, but I don't recall her ever being in a double act?

Gurpreet   Laurel and Hardy.

Aunty 5   Oh, well, I'm not sure if I can take that as a compliment.

Gurpreet   Please do.

Aunty 2   She is saying we are funny, not that we fat and skinny.

Aunty 5   Yes, but if it were the case then I'd …

Aunty 2 *gives her a hard look.*

… like to welcome you to your new home. After tea we'll show you around and Rhani will go over all the house rules …

Gurpreet   I'm sorry?

Aunty 2   You not worry, Rhani is a nice woman.

Gurpreet   I am not staying.

Aunty 2   But you have suitcase …

Aunty 5   And your husband …

Gurpreet   I came to return your beautiful bird and your DVD.

Gurpreet *hands the DVD to* **Aunty 2**.

Aunty 5   Is that all?

Aunty 2   There is always room here for benjis that need help.

Gurpreet *smiles and shakes her head.*

Gurpreet   Auntijies, thank you, but you should save the room for someone who does.

Gurpreet *places the bird cage on the table.*

I am no longer in my cage.

The **Aunties** *smile and nod.*

Aunty 2   Did the movie help?

Gurpreet   I didn't watch it.

Beat.

Aunty 5   Maybe next time you're passing, we could all watch it … Together?

Gurpreet *smiles warmly then exits.*

As **Gurpreet** *leaves, the front door is left open and a yellow glow appears.*

Gurpreet *stands looking at the blue sky, smiling to herself.*

Blackout.

Author's Postscript

Women's Refuge

Taken from personal experience, and a woman's refuge has been consulted for research. This information is only used to highlight any relevant issues.

Vulnerable Adults

The Raj scenario is based upon true case studies of a growing number of British Asian families who have family members with learning disabilities and personality disorders. Some are unable to cope or some choose not to. In these cases the family members with the disability are either abused, as they are unable to communicate, or victims like Gurpreet are innocently brought over to care for them. Many brought over do not speak English, and have no support network or anywhere to turn: who will hear their story? I hope this story will be heard and make a difference.

The Autistic Spectrum

Impairments of social interaction, communication and imagination, and a narrow, repetitive pattern of activity.

Forced Marriage

When one or both spouses do not consent to the marriage and some element of duress is involved. Duress includes both physical and emotional pressure.

www.ingramcontent.com/pod-product-compliance
Ingram Content Group UK Ltd.
Pitfield, Milton Keynes, MK11 3LW, UK
UKHW020730020325
455688UK00017B/338